Inclusion

Inclusion

The Dream and the Reality
Inside Special Education

Jeanne D'Haem

ROWMAN & LITTLEFIELD
Lanham • Boulder • New York • London

Published by Rowman & Littlefield
A wholly owned subsidiary of The Rowman & Littlefield Publishing Group, Inc.
4501 Forbes Boulevard, Suite 200, Lanham, Maryland 20706
www.rowman.com

Unit A, Whitacre Mews, 26-34 Stannary Street, London SE11 4AB

British Library Cataloguing in Publication Information Available

Library of Congress Cataloging-in-Publication Data Available

Names: D'Heam, Jeanne
Title: Inclusion : The dream and the reality inside special education / Jeanne D'Heam.
Description: Lanham : Rowman & Littlefield, 2016. | Includes bibliographical references.
ISBN 9781498524865 (cloth : alk. paper) | ISBN 9781475824872 (paper : alk. paper) | ISBN 9781498524889 (electronic)

Printed in the United States of America

Contents

Foreword

Madeleine Will

This book is complex and surprising. It is part absorbing memoir full of enriched wisdom, part collection of evocative portraits of characters and events that move with the pace of a film or television series, and part compelling narrative of a social history that is largely unknown and unheralded in our country.

Jeanne D'Haem, a distinguished special educator, beautifully writes it; it is poignant and insightful, wry at times and hilarious at others. But most fascinating is the clever and creative organization of its pieces that together provide a greater grasp of how a determined and quietly brave teacher and administrator could help transform a society with one radical idea—that children with disabilities could learn and develop knowledge and skills, could *benefit* from education.

For the millions of Americans who are individuals with a disability, who have a family member who is disabled, or are professionals who work with and on behalf of persons with disability, the origin of the disability rights revolution in the United States is familiar. In the post–World War II period, particularly, parents began to choose with greater and greater frequency not to place their child or adult child with a disability in an institution that specialized in the care of such persons. Such parents and families increasingly believed that isolating individuals from a nurturing family and from their community was an unacceptable, even repugnant path.

As more and more families rejected institutionalization for their family members, political and social pressure built for education and other services and supports to emerge in communities for people with disabilities where more and more resided. In the 1970s, a series of court cases, most notably the *Pennsylvania Association for Retarded Citizens (PARC) v. Commonwealth of Pennsylvania* lawsuit led to the passage of a federal law guaranteeing the right to education for children with disabilities, the Education of All Handicapped Children Act of 1975, now known as the Individuals with Disabilities Education Act (IDEA), which celebrated its fortieth anniversary in 2015.

But what came next, had to come next in order to make the law meaningful. D'Haem illuminates the painstaking, often trial-and-error invention of a system of education for students with disabilities in a society that clearly did not comprehend, and to some extent resisted, the marked and pervasive change that the IDEA signified. As this book reveals, the process of invention was purposeful and sustained, but not rapid or orderly, and it offers the caution that legislative prescription often runs smack into the vagaries of human institutions, not to mention human will and spirit.

The chapters align problems related to a particular child or family with the evolving understanding of thinking and practice as the field of special education evolved over the decades of D'Haem's experience. From separate schools for special education students to the inclusion of students with disabilities in regular schools and school-wide activities, from separate, self-contained classes in schools to general education classes, from maladapted school discipline policies to more enlightened procedures acknowledging the relationship between behavior and disability, the reader follows along with fascination on one discerning woman's journey through a historical unfolding of immense importance to Americans then and now.

NOTE

Madeleine Will, was the assistant secretary for the Office of Special Education and Rehabilitative Services during the Reagan administration. Madeline promoted the regular education initiative, and other transition programs. She recently founded the Collaboration to Promote Self-Determination (theCPSD.org).

Preface

Every morning parents drop their children off at school. Students amble in and the doors close behind them. The school yard, so noisy just a minute ago, is silent. Have you ever wondered what happens inside? How does the principal deal with the boy down your street who calls other children stupid and retarded? What happens to that little girl who sings and talks at home but won't say a word to anyone else, ever?

You have already seen the classrooms, the art room, and the gym. This book will take you into the principal's office, when the door is closed and she is calling the police or the district attorney. It reveals how teachers, psychologists, administrators, and members of the board of education decide what to do about children with special needs, behind the closed doors of private meetings.

Children with problems are a special interest of mine, because I was a child with a problem. I am left-handed. Only 10 percent of people have this trait. Today this is considered a possible sign of creativity and even athletic ability. Recent presidents Gerald Ford, George Bush, Bill Clinton, and Barak Obama are left-handed. Ronald Reagan was born left-handed, but he was taught to write with his right hand like many in the late 1940s and early 1950s. At that time left-handedness was thought to be a severe impediment.

Sir Cyril Bert wrote that left-handed people are fumblers and bunglers who flounder about like fish out of water in his book, *The Backward Child*. Ten years later, in 1947, Adam Blau disparaged left-handedness as infantile negativism that led to stubbornness, superstition, and other traits such as obsessive behaviors. He was the head of child psychiatry at Mount Sinai Hospital in New York.

"Turning" a left-handed child was considered the duty of responsible parents. My father had me practice writing with my right hand night after night, but the next day I naturally used my left hand. He became angry at what he considered my stubborn refusal to obey. He began to slap the left side of my face whenever he saw me using my left hand. The repeated blows made me deaf in my left ear.

Throughout my life I have questioned well-meaning attempts to change or label attributes considered bad or wrong in children. As a teacher and school administrator, I have been committed to providing educational opportunities for children, despite any personal or physical differences. I wrote *Inclusion: The Dream and the Reality Inside Special Edu-*

cation to show the efforts teachers and administrators make to educate students who are different.

Schools in the United States have a unique quality that is practically unknown in the rest of the world. No child can be turned away from a public school. Education is a property right under the law. No one can take your car or your home away from you without just cause, and no one can deny a child the right to an education without very good reasons. Expulsion is very rare. A student would have to bring a gun to school or sell drugs on school property in order to be permanently excluded.

Administrators and teachers must somehow find the right place and program for everyone. They work with sex offenders, faith healers, and give lessons about exactly where to put on a condom. Schools take the tired and poor, the homeless, those who are here illegally, and even the dangerous. These students can lower test scores, because they don't speak English, or they don't speak at all. Some won't sit still while others are slow to learn. However, no matter what their problems are, teachers work with everyone. Recently Hillary Clinton mentioned this little known fact about our schools. I feel we should be proud of this accomplishment.

The first chapter will introduce you to Sara who was a hydrocephalic. Due to a blockage of spinal fluid, her head had swelled to the size of a pumpkin and she could never move from the pillows that supported her. In those days, an educational program was considered to be impossible for her and she never left the institution where she had been left by her parents.

I forgot about Sara for almost thirty years until I interviewed the student president at a county community college. Ellen's face was fresh and lovely with perfectly spaced eyes and nose. Her clear skin contrasted with the dark hair she had tossed into a ponytail. I was meeting with college students during a site visit for the National Down Syndrome Society as a member of their grant selection committee. Based on interviews and other information, selection committee members would award a substantial grant to develop an on-campus program for individuals with Down syndrome and other developmental delays.

Ellen told the members of the grant committee about her plans to work in a day care center after she graduated. She casually shared that she had been born with hydrocephalus and had two shunts to drain the fluid from her brain. Her parents had been advised to put her into an institution, but they had refused and she had attended special education classes in her local school district. Suddenly, I remembered Sara's prison and underneath my glasses, both eyes burned with tears. Quietly I sucked them into my mouth so no one would see.

Perhaps a decade from now, stereotypes about Attention Deficit Disorder (ADD) will change as stereotypes about left-handed people changed. Students with ADD will be seen as active learners and their hyperactivity will be channeled instead of medicated. I once discussed hyperactivity with the superintendent of a large school district. He admitted he had ADD, but said he could never do his job without it!

As a school administrator I have confronted an important challenge; reaching every single student, black, white, indifferent, or frightened. This is the secret strength and wonder of the American educational system. No other country even makes an attempt to accomplish this. It is time that the American public is aware of the miracles taking place in the public school down the street. This book takes you into the confidential conferences among psychologists, principals, and teachers as they struggle to provide a program for every single child. The door to the school is open to everyone.

All of the events in this book are true. Names, identifying details, and places have been changed, but the situation, the confusion, and the struggles really happened. I used my own name, Jeanne, throughout the book to highlight what administrators have learned over four decades of change. How did we get from Sara in Belchertown to Ellen in college? Let me be your guide through decades of change. This transition has been a revolution in our schools but we have crossed a threshold and we will never go back.

It takes a lot of time and thought to find the right program for a child who is different; however, every single child is important. I chose to work with children with special needs, because I am left-handed and partially deaf. I am also just as stubborn as predicted.

Acknowledgments

I would like to thank the students with special needs and families I have come to know and respect. They taught me that what might seem like a disaster can turn out to be quite wonderful. They have been an inspiration to me that never ends. My husband, Bruce Stein, and my daughter, Jennifer Kobrin, have listened to my stories over the years and supported my writing. Colleagues Irene VanRiper, Peter Griswold, Erika DeBruine, Rodney Williams, Danna Ethan, Laura Weitzman, Jean Crichton, Gayle Carrick, and Marcy Craver offered important and helpful feedback as well as support for this project.

Introduction

Inclusion: The Dream and the Reality Inside Special Education reveals the secrets of how problems have been addressed over four decades of efforts to include students with special needs in public schools. This book traces the history of special education in a typical school, the one around the corner from you. The book begins in institutions for the disabled, which were once considered the best places to protect people with disabilities. Individuals had a safe place to live, and families were told the burden of care should be left to professionals. Unfortunately, institutions ended up overcrowded and underfunded. Protection turned into neglect.

Chapter 1 will introduce you to children who lived in institutions and the caring staff who struggled to provide basic care. When getting everyone dressed each day was difficult, educational programs were considered impossible.

A few courageous families began to defy the professional advice of the times, and kept their children home where they could be loved. Public schools began to create self-contained special education classes. Chapter 2 reveals that questions about an appropriate curriculum for students with developmental disabilities rapidly emerged. Should schools teach sex education to students with disabilities? Parents, and teachers, were challenged to consider this idea.

Dreadful conditions inside institutions were the catalyst for the procedural protections mandated in the Individuals with Disabilities Education Act (IDEA). Parents were given the right to disagree with programs offered by public schools. Chapter 3 illustrates complex or even amusing issues that can arise when parents and professionals disagree.

The IDEA lists specific classification categories for children with special needs; however, some children do not fit in any category. Chapter 4 demonstrates the lengths that dedicated teachers will go to get special services for children who don't find a place in established categories.

Moving students with developmental disabilities and autism spectrum disorder into classes with normally developing peers is a positive change. However, misunderstandings will occur. Chapters 5 and 7 divulge how potential disasters due to accusations of drug use and violence were averted.

Over the years, awareness of the benefits of integration grew. Administrators quickly saw that even children with profound disabilities could benefit other children and teachers in a school. Public schools are now committed to providing an appropriate education for every child, no matter what challenges are present. Protecting students, including those with special needs, from intruders, sex offenders, or bullying are topics in chapters 6, 8, and 9.

The final story in chapter 10 describes how a parent helped teachers to see that too much protection was almost as bad as not enough protection. Students with disabilities need to make mistakes and learn to solve problems on their own. Self-determination is the new challenge in special education.

ONE

Belchertown State Institution for the Feeble-Minded

For nearly six years I had no concepts whatsoever of nature or mind or death or God. I literally thought with my body. Without a single exception, my memories of that time are tactual. . . . I was like an unconscious clod of earth. Then suddenly . . . I awoke to language, to knowledge of love, to the usual concepts of nature, good and evil.
—Helen Keller

There was no way for the state coordinator of institutional schools to ignore the plaintive question, "Do you think you could find a school for me?" There was no one else in the dilapidated hallway outside the locked children's ward at Belchertown State Institution for the Feeble-Minded in western Massachusetts. In 1976, Jeanne, a coordinator for the Massachusetts Bureau of Institutional Schools, worked in several state institutions: Belchertown State Institution for the Feeble-Minded, Walter F. Fernald State School, Munson State Hospital, and Dever State School.

Her job was to find educational programs for the children who lived in the institutions. She had noticed Sara when she passed through the childrens' wards at Belchertown. However Jeanne never realized she could talk, thoughtlessly associating physical deformity with mental incapacity. Her first impulse was to mutter something reassuring about finding a school and hurry on to the meeting, but the lies would not come.

That innocent question had come from a twist of nature so wicked that one wondered how God could be so cruel. Sara had a severe case of hydrocephalus, and her head looked like a misshapen pumpkin. She had been left unattended in the hall because she didn't need to be locked up, Sara wasn't going anywhere, ever.

The brain sits in a bath of cerebrospinal fluid. When the ventricular system is blocked, fluid builds up, damages the brain, and results in an enlarged skull. Today a child born with hydrocephalus would have a shunt inserted to allow the fluids to drain normally. In those days such a treatment was unknown. Sara was probably ten years old, but she could not raise her head. It was at least three times larger than normal; the enlargement had wrenched and distorted her eyes, nose, and mouth. Her skin was lumpy and bulged in odd places. This sweet little girl did not even have the privacy offered by hair—wispy brown strands stuck up all over her head. Her follicles were stretched too far apart to add anything but another level of the grotesque.

Unable to sit up, Sara had called out to the coordinator's waist, the part of people she usually saw as they hurried by with mops, medications, or on their way to meetings. Her world was enclosed by the edges of a hospital gurney. If she moved from the support provided by the pillows, her neck would snap.

Sara had heard about Jeanne. She had discovered that plans were being made for children to attend schools outside of Belchertown, and she wanted to know if any plans were being made for her. Jeanne decided to be a few minutes late for her meeting since nobody ever came on time anyway, and leaned over the gurney so she could speak to Sara. She took her hand and held it while they talked.

Sara said that she wanted to ride on a school bus. She asked if the teachers read stories in school. She still remembered a lady who came to the ward and read a story. Most of all Sara wanted to make a card to send to her mother because she had not seen her all year. Jeanne listened in shame and frustration. Sara could speak and she could dream; however, there were no schools that could handle Sara's physical challenges even though she was quite capable of learning. Jeanne didn't know what to say or how to answer Sara. She just stood there looking into the sensitive brown eyes of a hopeful little girl who was a prisoner of her own head. At this time, there was no way that Sara could get on a bus or get out of this dreary institution even for one afternoon.

"I know that God has a purpose for me," Sara said finally sensing that there weren't any plans for her. "I just haven't found out what it is yet." Her eyes were full of determination. Sara turned her gaze toward the state-issued green paint peeling from the wall. Jeanne unlocked the dayroom door and walked in with her own head weighing heavily on her shoulders. It would take another twenty years for the U.S. Supreme Court in *Cedar Rapids Community School v. Garret* to rule that medical care, and even transport by an ambulance and skilled nursing care, was a child's legal right and had to be provided when it was essential for a child to attend school. Sara was dead long before that.

Belchertown was built for the "feeble-minded" in 1922 and was closed in 1992 after the *Springfield Union News* published a series of articles that exposed the subhuman living conditions in damning detail. All of the children were finally moved twenty years after the 1976 efforts by the Bureau of Institutional Schools to get them out of the vacuous wards and into community school programs. Located on 845 isolated acres, a third of a mile away from the tiny hamlet of Belchertown, there are now plans to turn it into a park or a retirement community.

In Belchertown and the other state institutions, children were washed and fed, but they were not expected to learn or to make decisions for themselves. *Laggards in Our Schools*, published in 1915, was the first special education text; however, education for the severely retarded was seen as a waste of resources. In 1934, children with an IQ below fifty were legally excluded from school. The Ohio Court of Appeals ruled that "as a matter of common sense it is apparent that a moron of very low type, or an idiot, or imbecile is incapable of absorbing knowledge (and) . . . ought to be excluded" (*Board of Education of Cleveland Heights v. State*).

The Berkshire Mountains seemed to be sighing at their own beauty on the days that Jeanne was assigned to visit Belchertown. The corner of Berkshire Avenue and Apple Street turned onto the winding drive that led to the massive buildings.

Driving down the long driveway, you could hear the screaming. The long and well-practiced screams reached around the barren rooms and got caught in the corners. The echoes slithered underneath the flimsy mattresses on the long rows of sagging iron beds and stuck in people's ears until they didn't hear them anymore. The screams started low, grew into a painful peak, and then dropped into silence.

"Why do they scream like that?" Jeanne asked attendants in the day-room. "Nobody is hurting them."

"Bored, I guess," was the best answer she heard. Maybe it gets some adrenaline going, she thought. Screaming could feel pretty good if there was absolutely nothing else to do. Maybe a good long shriek is the only way some children can show that they are alive; the only decision they can make is when to start and when to stop.

Jeanne had gotten used to the smell of urine, and even the diapers that were used to tie many children into chairs, but she never got used to the wailing. At that time she was young, energetic, naïve, and inexperienced. Her job as a state coordinator was to get as many children as she could out of Belchertown and other state institutions.

Dorothea Dix spoke to the Massachusetts Legislature in 1843 about the pitiful state of insane people she found in jails and poorhouses throughout the state. "I proceed, Gentlemen, briefly to call your attention to the present state of Insane Persons confined within this Common-wealth, in cages, stalls, pens! Chained naked, beaten with rods, and lashed into obedience" (*New World Encyclopedia*).

As a result asylums and training schools were established from 1850 to 1930 on the assumption that retarded individuals were a menace and needed to be removed from the general population so they would not reproduce. In 1927, the Supreme Court Justice Oliver Wendell Holmes Jr. ruled that forced sterilization was legal and famously declared, "Three generations of imbeciles are enough." The Supreme Court has never expressly overturned this ruling (*Carrie Buck v. John Hendren Bell, Superintendent of State Colony for Epileptics and Feeble Minded*).

As Jeanne paused in front of the elegant granite entrance, a blue jay flew from the overgrown holly bushes to the slate roof and back again. His insistent cries warned the chipmunks, gray squirrels, and the tiny voles that she was an invader. She felt like an invader too. The attendants looked up and watched carefully whenever "that state woman" walked through the dayrooms. They knew Jeanne had been hired to get children out of the institution and away from their care. It seemed that every request she made was countered with an icy, "We are doing the best we can here."

In 1971, parents in the Pennsylvania Association for Retarded Children brought a class action suit against the Commonwealth of Pennsylvania for its failure to provide all school-age children, even those who were considered retarded, with access to a public education. The court ruled that all children in Pennsylvania between the ages of six and twenty-one were to be provided with a publicly supported education.

In Massachusetts, a similar suit was brought by Ben Ricci, the father of a mentally retarded boy at Belchertown, and was joined by advocacy groups for the retarded. The courtroom testimony revealed practices in the institutions that were so indefensible that District Court Judge Joseph Tauro ordered the court to take over the Massachusetts system of education for the mentally retarded. Tauro ruled that the department of education had done nothing. He saw no way that it would ever comply with the law without total supervision.

Judge Tauro ordered that full evaluations, comprised of medical, psychological, educational, related services, and social history evaluations, be completed on every child under the age of twenty-one who lived in an institution. He instructed Peg Pyne, director of the Bureau of Institutional Schools, to document the needs of the children. The facts would help to convince the state legislature to appropriate funding to establish proper educational facilities.

In 1976 the Massachusetts Bureau of Institutional Schools hired Jeanne as a program coordinator. Her assignment was to gather background information on each of the twenty-five children on her caseload, try to find the parents, arrange for evaluations, advise the client and his or her parents of their legal rights, and coordinate the development of an educational program. Jeanne was assigned to five of the institutions for the mentally retarded established by W. E. Fernald in 1922. Belchertown and Munson State School were located in western Massachusetts. Fernald State School near Boston, was first established in 1848 by Samuel Howe whose wife, Julia Ward Howe wrote the *Battle Hymn of the Republic* and founded the Girl Scouts. It was initially called the Experimental School for Teaching and Training Idiotic Children.

Dever State School was originally a military staging area where German prisoners of war were housed. After World War II it was turned into a school for the mentally disabled. Wrentham State School was established in 1906 to train the mentally disabled so they could be returned to society. However, in 1973 the school's certification was revoked. Federal Judge Joseph Tauro visited and reported it was a disgrace and a nightmare. The new superintendent at Wrentham had a goal to find a bed for every patient. Jeanne's goal was to get children out of the institution or at least into special classes in schools near the hospitals.

By 1977, politicians in Massachusetts were eager to close the large institutions in a movement called deinstitutionalization. In reality they also hoped to find less expensive solutions. That was the challenge coordinators faced. No one had a clue of how to do it—or even anyone to ask.

Days in institutions unfolded like an empty paper bag. There was nothing inside them. There was only one shape it could take, unless it was ripped apart by dramatic events. Children wandered aimlessly back and forth in empty rooms dragging their feet in the Thorazine shuffle. There were no toys, no stuffed animals to comfort the children. Bedrooms lined dark hallways, which ended in large dayrooms. Children were not allowed back into the bedrooms during the day. The dayroom windows were too high for most children to see the outside. They were covered with bars. Chairs were lined up all around the walls of the room and a television blared loudly all day long. Many times there was no picture, only a fuzzy screen. Many children sat in the straight-backed wooden chairs rocking back and forth.

"Why don't you have any couches?" Jeanne asked. The matron explained that the hospital administration didn't want to see the residents sitting around all day long. When asked why there were no toys, she explained that the children don't know what to do with toys; they just break them. "If you give kids like this a crayon, they will just eat it," she said.

It seemed like a waste of resources and time to conduct evaluations of children who had nothing; no books, no crayons, not even blocks to stack. The needs were obvious to anyone who witnessed the half-naked children lying on the filthy dayroom floor. Some toys and a teacher for fifteen minutes a day would have improved things dramatically. However, the law mandated a comprehensive evaluation before services could be provided. No evaluation, no services. What evaluation could be more powerful than the sight of a child left in a corner?

The evaluation for each child began with a visit to the records' vault. The files were kept in the basement of the administration building and were carefully guarded by suspicious matrons. Despite written permission to see the medical history on each of the children, it was as if Jeanne had asked for the original Dead Sea Scrolls. Alarmed by the request, the matron in charge at Belchertown called the superintendent's office to ask what this was all about. With his permission, she slowly retrieved each of the files requested and Jeanne was sharply informed that she was not allowed to take them out of the building. Since there was no place to sit, she balanced the green oak tag files on the narrow counter and carefully turned the onionskin papers so they would not fall out onto the worn tile floor. Most of the carbon copies were difficult to read especially in the dim light of the single hanging bulb.

Jeanne wondered if anyone had ever referred to the files before. The musty disorganized contents were written in another language. One child had autosomal trisomy of group G, E, or D. Another had lipid histiocytosis of kerasin type and had extensive testing from several hospitals to prove it. (A note explained that lipid histiocytosis was actually Gaucher's disease.) In addition to the autosomal trisomy of group G, the records listed secondary conditions like porencephaly or malformations of the gyri. One of the children had anencephaly. The medical information was so obscure and useless that it started to seem funny. What was acute infantile diffuse sclerosis or Krabbe's disease! Perhaps something could be done to help a crabby child.

Even when the diagnosis was understandable, Jeanne wondered what could be done with the information. The records seemed like they were written to justify hopelessness. Most records began with hospital reports from the day of birth, and included cryptic notes such as "advised parents to institutionalize immediately."

The spaces between the lines held the drama much like the pauses between the notes in a symphony. Desperate parents consulted one specialist after another, as they tried to understand trigeminal cerebral angiomatosis. They wanted a baby to love and nurture, called Bobby or Susan. They wanted a cure, a medicine. The experts gave them medical etiology that implied they should not get involved; this is too complicated for you.

When advised to put the baby into an institution where he or she could be "protected and properly cared for," records showed that many parents faithfully visited for years, but eventually stopped. The director explained that visits usually tapered off when the children developed secondary sexual characteristics. Parents who were able to deal with a young child recoiled at beards or breasts. After ten or twelve years in an institution, most of the children's tests and medical records became scanty and hard to follow. It seemed as though the children had been slowly forgotten—even by the institutions that cared for them. Jeanne gave the records back; she had a different job to do.

She hired a pediatrician from a nearby town to perform independent medical examinations of several children. Dr. Marzak was all business with closely cropped hair and round glasses. He was methodical, highly organized, and unemotional. Jeanne arranged to use an examining room on a Saturday and scheduled appointments for the children on her caseload who resided at Belchertown. Dr. Marzak would send their blood and urine samples off to a lab at the end of the day and write up his medical report. It was one part of the comprehensive evaluation mandated for each child by Judge Tauro under IDEA.

An attendant led Edward into the small office the institution staff had found for the physicals. Edward was fifteen years old and his records indicated that he had been diagnosed with profound mental retardation or an IQ score under twenty. Edward was unresponsive during the exam. He did not appear frightened or interested, did not respond to questions, and mainly stared vacantly into space. When Dr. Marzak finished his examination, he helped Edward off of the desk he was using as an examining table to observe his gait and any ataxia or lack of muscle coordination.

Edward held on to the wooden desk, his long stringy legs were all knees, and he was very unsteady on his feet. However, he responded when asked if he wanted to leave and immediately peered slowly around the room, as if he were looking for something. He reached for the wall and inched along, using it for support.

A recent physical therapy evaluation report by the hospital staff revealed that although Edward had proper gait, he was gradually losing the ability to walk due to severe muscle weakness. The therapist had recommended a minimum of fifteen minutes of physical therapy each day, but there were no physical therapists assigned to his ward so he had never received any physical therapy.

The attendant came to take him back up to the dayroom, and Jeanne followed to get an idea of Edward's ward routine. When the hospital attendant tied Edward into a chair with a diaper, she asked why he had to be restrained. Edward moved too slowly to run around and cause trouble.

"The minute you turn your back he runs to the bathroom," the attendant explained.

"Why is that such a problem?"

"He sticks his head in the toilet and drinks whatever is in it. He won't stop, so we have to keep him in restraints."

"Can't he be trained not to do that?"

"We don't have the staff to watch him all the time. We are doing the best we can around here," he said. He patted Edward on the shoulder and looked reproachfully at Jeanne. The hospital staff felt as though they were being evaluated. They were aware of the lack of services and were angry that new evaluations were being conducted when they already knew what services would be helpful.

Dr. Marzak called Jeanne at home at 7:30 on Monday morning and was quite agitated in contrast to his dispassionate demeanor two days ago. "The saline content in Edward's blood is much too high," he said. "The lab redid the tests for me because he has the saline level of a dead person."

"What?"

"Jeanne," he answered, "Edward's salt content is so high that he has to be dead, technically. I already called the unit and gave them a piece of my mind about this. They have been restricting his fluids. They were pretty mad about my interference, but they already agreed to allow normal fluids. I hope we did something for the poor kid."

Jeanne had never bothered to interview the ward staff about Edward and had not suspected any neglect or mistreatment on the ward. Shocked and upset, she went back to the ward to talk to them that very day.

The ward staff nurse was quite indignant and defensive about the phone call from Dr. Marzak. She explained (loudly) that Edward was a "ruminator." He would bring up food from his stomach, play with it in his mouth and with his hands before he licked it off and swallowed it again. Rumination, biting themselves, picking at the skin, pulling their hair out, pushing on the eyelid were common self-stimulatory behaviors of children in institutions. In an effort to curtail the rumination, a hospital staff doctor had ordered reduced liquids.

Four years and many staff changes later, no one had rescinded the order or questioned it. Edward's fluids had been restricted for so long that he was, technically, dead. No wonder he had to be restrained or he would drink out of the toilet! The daily restraints left him with no muscle tone so he was losing the ability to walk.

After all the evaluations were completed, the individual educational plan for Edward recommended physical therapy and occupational therapy, but there were no schools that would accept a child who threw up in order to have something to play with. Although he was on the list for both services at Belchertown, it is doubtful that any services were ever provided.

As a case coordinator for the Bureau of Institutional Schools, Jeanne was assigned to work with children in state institutions throughout Massachusetts. Fernald is located about ten miles from Boston in the suburban community of Waltham that had grown up around it. The Fernald School is the oldest institution of its kind in the country. At its peak, some 2,500 people were confined there, most of them children. All of them were called feeble-minded, whether they were or not. The Fernald Center, originally called the Massachusetts School for Idiotic Children, was founded by reformer Samuel Gridley Howe in 1848 with a $2,500 appropriation from the Massachusetts State Legislature. The school eventually comprised seventy-two buildings, located on 196 acres. The Fernald School, and others like it, was part of a popular American movement in the early twentieth century called the Eugenics movement. The idea was to separate people considered to be genetically inferior from the rest of society, to prevent them from reproducing.

Joseph lived down a long dirty hallway in one of the oldest buildings in Fernald. He was mainly catatonic. He would assume a certain pose and sit motionless, often with his index finger pointing up into the air and inclined slightly toward his nose. Jeanne didn't know what she could do for Joseph. He had been placed on an adult ward because there was no more room on any of the children's units. Some of the men there must have been fifty, but it was hard to tell. There was no forward motion in the lives of the patients who lived in the back wards. Faces in front of minds that have no reason to function do not develop wrinkles. The skin remains as smooth as our uncomprehending backsides.

Joseph was basically long and bony with high cheekbones under empty brown eyes. He never looked directly at anything or anyone. He would tilt his head and stare out of the corner of his eyes when someone threw a chair or lay on the floor kicking. Joseph was often lying across several wooden chairs and draped in a ragged sheet. There were few visitors at Fernald and little reason to make sure that everyone got dressed.

"Clothing carts come from the laundry in the morning," Kathy, the day nurse and unit supervisor explained. "Unfortunately, most of the time we don't get enough clothes for everyone. The patients who get to the cart first, get clothes and we have some pretty aggressive ones here. They put kids like Joseph on the adult wards but they don't send us proper sizes. Besides, Joseph doesn't care," she sighed. Kathy sat in the nursing station behind a sliding glass panel. She had round cheeks, round eyes, and used a lot of bobby pins to keep her white hat perched on unruly brown hair. Her finger had grown fat around her wedding ring, and it looked like it would not come off anymore. Papers and medicine bottles were arranged by height in rows on the shelves behind her desk.

"What if I ask his father to send some clothes for him?" Jeanne suggested.

"All clothing goes to the laundry," she explained firmly. "We don't have the staff to go sorting out stuff on this ward," she said reaching up to close the glass panel. "We do not have the staff," she reiterated, her voice rising, so everyone could hear. "There are no private possessions on this ward." No one in this ward went anywhere, or would ever go anywhere, so clothes were not important. For those who lived here; it was the only place on earth.

Eventually it was no longer an event when Jeanne stopped by on her weekly rounds. Kathy would look up from her desk when she opened the door and go back to whatever she was arranging, with the slightest acknowledgment.

Jeanne never got any acknowledgment from Joseph either. He didn't talk, didn't move, and didn't seem to care about anything around him. She didn't think she could do anything with him and her trips to observe him got shorter and became infrequent. Once, feeling guilty since she had not seen Joseph in several weeks, Jeanne came in the early evening, even though it was late. The shadows of the hard wooden ward chairs stretched across the dayroom, and Kathy had gone home.

Jock, the night attendant, was amused that someone like Joseph actually had a visitor. He had a gentle demeanor and large black hands on the end of spidery arms. He asked if Jeanne wanted to see a trick. "Hey Joe," he called out in a warm tenor voice, "wanna cigarette?" Jock waved his open pack in the air, rustling the cellophane. Joseph smiled and tilted his head to look at the pack of cigarettes. He got up off the row of chairs he was laying across, ambled over, and followed the waving cigarette pack with his eyes. Then he reached out and pulled a cigarette out with a perfect pincer grasp. Jeanne's surprise at his finger dexterity quickly turned to amazement when Joseph put the whole cigarette in his mouth, and chewed.

Jock beamed at her gasp. With lips barely closed, Joseph calmly chewed the tobacco, paper, and filter. He finally swallowed the stringy mass and Jeanne almost gagged. Jock's grin revealed large white teeth, and even Joseph had a wisp of a smile and a knowing look. Both of these naughty boys clearly enjoyed shock and disapproval. They had a thing going on and probably had demonstrated this little scene to Kathy and other visitors.

Jeanne decided then and there that Joseph was going to school. If intelligence could be gauged by an ability to torment the teacher, this young man was a prodigy! Based on that performance, he deserved to be in a school program where he could tease teachers on a regular basis. "How would you like to go to school, Joe?" she asked. Jock's eyes got very big, and the whites matched the teeth in his open mouth. Joe pointed his finger at his nose and Jeanne accepted that answer as positive.

She knew that a school district in Peabody had recently opened a class for children who had severe developmental delays, and Joseph fit that category. The class only had a few students, and the district might be interested in the tuition money. The state would pay the school district to provide a program for Joseph to attend. Peabody was a long way away, but there was also money to pay for his transportation.

"Joe, do you think you could get dressed every day?" Jeanne asked the back of his head as he wandered back to stretch out on several of the chairs along the wall. "You have to get dressed if you want to go to school." Joe was clearly capable of learning. He had been living in a place without fun, without anything to play with, and he had invented his own little toy.

In the aftermath of World War II and the slaughter of Jews and those with mental retardation based on Nazi notions of racial purity, the U.S. Supreme Court ruled against separate institutions in *Brown vs. the Board of Education*: "education . . . is a right which must be made available to all on equal terms." This ruling was intended to end racial segregation, but it had an even greater effect on children with disabilities. Parents were no longer told to forget they ever had a child with mental retardation. They raised them at home and demanded services in the community for them. Local schools had to create special classes.

The director of special education in Peabody was willing to let Joe attend as a tuition student. Mike O'Reilly, the building principal, was Boston Irish through and through. "Let the poor kid give it a try," he said with an expansive wave. A school bus would pick up Joseph each morning and take him to the Peabody Elementary School.

Excited at her success in arranging a placement, Jeanne skipped through the underground tunnels that connected the Fernald buildings and ran up the stairs to Joseph's adult ward. When she told Kathy the good news, the nurse's round eyes became little slits. "We can't go running around after one patient all morning trying to get him dressed by 8:00."

"Nobody else is going anywhere, why can't you get Joseph dressed and ready for the bus?"

"He needs to learn how to dress himself. That's what he needs to learn. Why send somebody to school when they can't even get themselves dressed? You are just going to overwhelm him with that long bus ride and a strange place."

"Kathy, if we wait until can dress himself, he'll never go anywhere, will he?" Jeanne replied.

"Sometimes we run out of Dilantin toward the end of the month," Kathy continued to argue. "He could have a seizure. I can't guarantee that the morning aides will have time to get his meds before he has to leave. What if the cart from the pharmacy is late?" she insisted. "What do you expect me to do then? I'm responsible for him, and I can't allow this child to leave the institution and risk having a seizure." Jeanne didn't respond. "It's not safe for him to be off of the hospital grounds; he could have a seizure," Kathy repeated satisfied that she had protected her patient.

"I think it would be more dangerous for Joe to spend the rest of his life here on the ward," Jeanne told her. At that, Kathy got up out of her chair and left the nursing station to complain about the total disregard for the safety of her patient; however, the assistant director gave a special order so that Joseph's seizure medication would be given to him early enough so that he could take the bus.

Joseph's first day of school was scheduled for a Tuesday so Jeanne could visit the ward on Monday and remind Kathy that he needed to be ready to get on the bus at eight o'clock. Anxious that she would encounter passive resistance, Jeanne noted a tenuous air of interest in the project. Kathy slid open the glass panel.

"What time is that school bus coming?"

"Eight o'clock."

"Well, I don't know if I can get Joey ready by then. I'll have to get him dressed before anyone else."

Since she said, "I'll have to get him dressed" and was naming Joey, instead of just referring to "them," things looked promising.

"Joseph," Jeanne said to his vacant eyes and pointing finger, "you will like school. You have to get dressed tomorrow." No response. "I want you to do everything nurse Kathy says." A little drip of spittle ran out of the side of his mouth.

At 9:51 Tuesday morning Mike O'Reilly called Jeanne out of a meeting. He was agitated. He said that Joseph had to be carried off the bus and was sitting in a catatonic state in the classroom. "Hey," he said, "I like the kid, don't get me wrong, but I don't think he belongs here. He doesn't do anything." Jeanne convinced Mike that all the new sights and sounds and smells probably overwhelmed Joseph, since he had been in the institution for so long. He had probably never even been on a bus.

Mike agreed that perhaps that was the problem, and they decided to give Joseph a week and hold off until Friday on a decision. Jeanne would be able to get up to the school then and see Joseph in the classroom. On Wednesday when she called to see how things were going, Mike explained that Joseph had to be carried off the bus again and remained in a stiff catatonic state in the classroom. He was not eating and did not go to the bathroom. They discussed the possibility that Joseph might have been overmedicated, and Jeanne promised she would get over to the ward and talk to the staff.

On Thursday afternoon there was more bad news. There had been a fire drill that morning at the school, and Mr. O'Reilly had to carry Joseph out of the building and put him into his own car in the parking lot because he would not stand. "That individual is a danger to himself and to others," he said. "He needs to be in an institution hospital where he can be properly cared for!" It was time to give up; this had been a far-fetched idea from the beginning. It was already late afternoon, and Jeanne asked if Joseph could attend the next day so she would have time to cancel the bus and notify Kathy that Joseph would not need to get dressed for the rest of his life.

Jeanne's telephone rang the following morning. This time Mike O'Reilly's voice was animated and she could hear Joseph's classroom teacher in the background. It took a minute to understand, but Joseph had suddenly become "our boy." That morning Joseph had run off of the bus when it stopped in front of the school. He had raced inside and gone directly to his classroom. The door was open and "our boy" had gone in, located a puzzle on the shelf, and carefully carried it to his seat.

The teachers, secretaries, and even the custodians had come by to see the boy who had been catatonic for days, playing with a puzzle. Joseph's special education teacher thought he said something that sounded like "school." It was garbled, but she felt he was capable of speech and had called the director of special education to see about a speech therapist. Joseph never said Mama, and he never said Daddy. His first word was school. He drooled and would not look at anyone straight on, but he was alive; he wanted to do the most basic of human activities, he wanted to learn.

A few weeks later Jeanne went up to the ward in the late afternoon to see Joseph and ask how things were going. Kathy had gone home for the evening, but there was a scribbled picture carefully taped on the side of the sliding glass at the nursing station. The artist's name had been written on the bottom of the paper—Joseph. Jock was there in the fading light, hands resting lightly on his knees. "That Joe, he's talking now," he told her.

"Wow, what can he say?"

"He says 'school'—that's all he says—but," he noted with pride, "he says that very well."

David Perkins, of Harvard University, proposes that intelligence is learnable in his 1995 book *Outsmarting IQ*. He offers evidence that IQ changes over time in response to education, nutrition, and other influences. Perkins demonstrates that general knowledge and skill have a substantial impact on intelligent behavior and questions the theory that intelligence is a fixed attribute. He sees intelligence as mind-ware or the equipment of the mind; the pots and pans, egg beaters and corkscrews that enable people to cook something new out of the information at their disposal. When he was finally given the equipment, Joseph cooked up something new.

We don't know what happened to Sara or Joseph except that they sparked a revolution. Few people today would question that individuals with developmental disabilities can learn and respond to all kinds of stimulation. Parents are no longer told to put a child with developmental disabilities in an institution and forget they had a baby. There are supports and services in most cities and towns. Public schools are proud of the educational programs they offer to students with special needs. Colleges are starting programs for individuals with disabilities who want to take advantage of higher education. Improvements in medical science have helped children born with disabilities that would have been untreatable years before.

Like all revolutions, the idea of including children with differences in classes along with normally developing children has been fraught with difficulties, misunderstandings, and even fights. However, it would be unthinkable today to label a child as feeble-minded and to treat them as though they were incapable of learning.

Recently, a young mother of a five-year-old with Down syndrome and also named Joseph bragged, "My Joey can say bubbles. That's his main word right now but he says it very well." Her son has been in special programs since the day he was born. What words would Joseph have been able to say if he had special education services instead of lying on the floor at Fernald State for sixteen years? Hopefully not, "Can I have a cigarette?"

ESSENTIAL UNDERSTANDINGS

- Asylums and training schools were established from 1850 to 1930 on the assumption that, "despite their pathetic innocence, the retarded were a social menace and that segregation, not rehabilitation, was the answer." Various facilities to separate "idiots and lunatics not furiously mad" were established.
- Institutions were quickly overcrowded and underfunded.
- Many dedicated staff members did the best they could in poor conditions.
- Parents of individuals with developmental disabilities were responsible for the lawsuits in the 1970s that mandated an education for all children, regardless of the severity of their disability or where they lived.
- In Massachusetts a judge ordered that full evaluations, comprised of medical, psychological, educational, related services, and social history evaluations, be completed on every child under the age of twenty-one who lived in an institution. He instructed the newly created Bureau of Institutional Schools to document the needs of the children in institutions in order to convince the state legislature to appropriate funding to establish proper educational facilities.
- Documentation of disabilities was used to garner support for funding, but it emphasized problems not abilities and was a deficit approach.
- The trouble that Edward had with walking demonstrates that what appears to be obvious may be something else when all comprehensive evaluations are complete. Evaluation of all suspected areas of disability remains at the heart of the IDEA.

TWO

Sex Scandal

There are few presumptions in human relations more dangerous than the idea that one knows what another human being needs better than they do.
—Michael Ignatieff

Every school district has a secret pecking order. The math department sits at the top with the football program. Then comes science, English, history, languages, and finally physical education. High school teachers have more rank than middle school teachers, who have more than elementary school teachers. Less respected are the newcomers: physical education, sex education, and, finally, special education.

Sex education in schools has been hotly contested. Is this something that should be taught in school? Some contend that sex education curriculums encourage promiscuousness. In the 1980s opposition by members of the school board, as well as religious groups, defeated an initiative to require a sex-education curriculum in the New York Public Schools. New York City's Bloomberg administration mandated sex education in August 2011. In 2013 the birthrate among teenagers reached a new low of 10 percent.

Special education is also new. The Individuals with Disabilities Act became a federal law in 1975. It remains controversial even though it is not openly debated. No teacher or administrator wants to seem unsupportive of a child with a handicap. However, teachers who have classes of twenty-five students resent special education teachers who have eight.

Space is a problem in schools that were built before special education programs were mandated. Administrators resent giving full classrooms to special education teachers with six students. Students with special needs require special buses, special books, and special teachers. There are special rules for discipline.

15

The number of students eligible for special education has grown to 15 percent of school-age children. Board of education members and superintendents are often perplexed and confused by the myriad of costly programs needed for students classified as handicapped. They want to comply with the law and agree with the superintendent when additional staff members are needed, but this does not mean that special education staff members are welcome in the schools.

The first classes for students with developmental disabilities were usually housed in elementary schools. However, as these students grew older, this was no longer appropriate. Meeting the needs of young adults with disabilities was a struggle for special education administrators and teachers in the 1980s. There were many unanticipated problems.

Dressed in high heels and a dark blue suit, the new supervisor of special education, Jeanne, arrived at the district's administrative office. She was eager to start supervising something, but nobody seemed to know what to do with her. The superintendent was out of town, and the director of pupil personnel was in a meeting. His secretary sent her to the high school, but the high school principal was not available either. Elaine, his secretary, handed her a key with a quizzical look. "Special Ed. huh," she remarked with a frown.

Three floors up, Jeanne found the unmarked door at the end of the hall and the key turned in the lock. It opened to a small closet—was this supposed to be her office? There wasn't a window, only a flourescent light that blinked at jumbled piles of educational debris. Final exams spilled out of broken cardboard boxes, stacks of dated textbooks leaned precariously against the wall, and several old mimeograph machines sat in dusty desolation on the floor. Paint flaked off the ceiling and dusted the abandoned contents.

She had been hired as a new supervisor for special education in this suburban school district. She would monitor the district's compliance with the Individuals with Disabilities Education Act (IDEA), the federal law that mandated special education services for students with disabilities.

"The office you assigned me is full of old books and boxes of junk," she explained when Bruce, the high school principal, emerged from the coffee room with the football coach and two assistant principals. "There isn't even a desk or a chair."

"I told the science department to clean that out for you last week," he replied pulling his monogrammed shirt cuffs down over thick wrists. "That used to be the old copy room when we used spirit copiers. Now we have a copy center here in the main office." He proudly pointed out the spacious room with large windows as they walked by.

"The superintendent told me to find an office for you," Bruce said, "but we are overcrowded. I don't have any room for special education in my building. These kind of students don't belong in an academic high school—we don't know how to help them." Bruce was not a tall man, and he tended toward stocky, especially at the neck. His tightly buttoned shirt looked as if it were choking him. He acted like an army sergeant, all precision and bluster, but actually he lived with three cats.

Elaine, the head secretary, gave Jeanne a wire bin as a mailbox. The rest of the faculty had mail cubbies in alphabetical order. She put phone messages in the box since there was no other way to contact the supervisor of the special education department.

Each of the five district elementary schools had small classes for special education students. There were classes for children with communication problems, emotional problems, neurological impairments, and a very innovative preschool program.

In the middle school and the high school, students with learning disabilities, attended general classes and went to see a special education teacher in a resource center program for one or two periods a day. Rooms for resource classes were scarce. The special education teachers had to share rooms with general education teachers.

When the science teacher had a prep period, the special education teacher would meet her students in that room. Books and supplies all had to be schlepped and removed when class was over. Some teachers had to walk from one end of the building to the other to get to their next room. Occasionally students with special needs got into trouble when the teacher arrived at the classroom after they did.

Simply put, public school districts are less than eager to have children with special needs enrolled. Principals prefer musicians, cheerleaders, or computer geeks. They are especially partial to athletes. Bruce wanted trophies for his wall, and he put a lot of effort and money into making that happen. The dry cleaning bill for the football uniforms topped the budget for special education supplies.

Later that week, Bruce was walking down the hall picking up discarded papers on the way to his office. Jeanne stopped him. "Bruce," she said, "I need a telephone line, I can't do this job without a computer or even a phone."

"Jeanne, they have to run a line all the way up to the third floor from here," he said. "They have to drill though brick and asbestos. Can't you use the phone in the science office?"

"Herb is not very happy about me using his office," she told him. "I don't have a key and the door is locked unless he is in there. I can't have confidential conversations about special education students with the science teachers sitting around having coffee."

Bruce retorted by demanding to know why so much time and money was wasted on special education kids. "They aren't ever going to do anything, Jeanne. What's the point?"

"The point is, it's the law," she replied referring to the IDEA.

"Oh yeah?" he said his round face getting red. "We got so many laws now, it's impossible to do the job." He turned to ask a girl with fluffy hair and a blue headband if she had a hall pass. Finally he turned back to her. "Okay, I'll see what's going on with the phone line," he conceded. "By the way, did you get back to that woman who is calling here all the time about her son? Elaine and the other secretaries can't keep taking all these messages."

"No, Bruce, I didn't get back to her, I don't have a phone."

"She says she wants a sex education class for her son," he peered down at her out of the corner of his eye. "Isn't her son retarded?" he said. "Teaching retarded people about sex! What will they think of next?" he snorted and retreated into his office.

Later that month when a phone was installed, Jeanne had second thoughts about her insistence on a phone line. Mrs. Tucci called to say her son wasn't learning anything in his private school. "None of the other children in his class can even talk," she said.

Teachers called to complain about the students and what the parents wanted for their children. The members of the diagnostic team called to complain about what the teachers and the parents wanted. Advocates called to schedule observations, and building principals called to ask if they had to allow the advocates into the buildings. They didn't want outsiders coming in to tell them what to do.

Robbie's mother had called several times to welcome the new supervisor of special education. She also shared concerns about son's growing sexual maturity. Robbie was nineteen years old with growing facial and pubic hair. His mother was concerned about some of his behaviors and requested a sex education program for him. Jeanne decided to go see the class and meet Robbie herself.

The developmental disabilities class for students aged fifteen to twenty-one was housed in an elementary school on what was considered the less desirable side of town. Robbie, Eddie, William, Jeff, Roseanne, and Becky had been in the self-contained class for students with developmental disabilities for many years.

Ellen, their teacher, welcomed the visit from her supervisor. "Nobody ever comes down here," she admitted. "The building principal has never come to observe me teach. I feel like I work in East Jibip and everybody else works here."

Roseanne looked like a combination of Roseanne Barr and Beethoven. Stringy dark hair fell into her face and covered mournful black eyes. She usually walked around with her chin on her chest, and she looked disfigured although she was actually athletic. She was eager to please, but sometimes she stood too close to people and wanted to touch them.

Robbie was no more than 5'2" and he waddled back and forth as if he had something in his pants. He was nineteen. Jeff was stocky, and left to his own devices, he would rock back and forth blinking furiously. He needed to be reminded to keep his generous lips closed and wipe his mouth otherwise a little stream of spittle would wend its way down the side of his chin. His pants were hooked up high and the belt buckled above his waist.

Becky had a full head of lush auburn curls, eyes that matched, and full lips. She was the most talkative of the group. Her father was French, and she had spent summers in Lyon with her grandmother as a child.

This self-contained class was located in the kindergarten wing even though the students were all fifteen years old or older. The kindergarten rooms had bathrooms, and it had been decided that students with developmental disabilities should use their own bathroom. The class had started when the students were young, and they had just stayed in the same room as they grew older and would eventually age out of special education services. Special education services for students with disabilities were mandated under the IDEA until they turned twenty-one or graduated from high school.

Robbie had many of the characteristics of a person with Down syndrome. His stubby arms and legs were planted on a round body. His eyes were small and slanted which gave his face an Asian appearance made more apparent because his hair was jet black and carefully cut. He was always fastidiously dressed in a white shirt and khaki pants; however, his neat clothing was marred because he constantly sucked on his undershirt. The neck of his shirt was usually stretched up over his chin and gathered into his mouth. Robbie liked to lie on the floor mats and rock while he listened to music. His favorite song was *Hi Ho, Hi Ho, and It's Off to Work We Go* from *Snow White and the Seven Dwarfs*.

His mother had explained that Robbie had been sneaking into her closet and taking her underpants from the dirty clothes basket. He would hide them under his pillow, and she had discovered him asleep with the panties on over his head. Robbie attended Mass each Sunday with his family and had been accepted by the congregation. Recently however, he had grabbed the woman sitting next to him in a passionate embrace during the "kiss of peace."

"People are afraid of him now, and I don't know what to do," Mrs. Klein said. "We have told him over and over not to do this, but I am afraid to take him to Mass anymore. Church is the only place he goes other than school."

Jeanne honestly didn't know what to do either, and wondered what the district's responsibility was for a student who had problems outside of school.

Ellen had worked with Robbie for six years and knew him well. Petite and sturdy, she was the kind of teacher who could stop misbehavior with a glance from across the room. Ellen's sable hair framed her narrow face and her quick black eyes worked as well on the back of her head as the front. She had a low voice and seemed to take most difficulties with a bemused smile. She was from the Midwest and often noted that things "could'a been worse."

Ellen was not surprised when she was informed about the conversation with Robbie's mother. "He has his hands inside his pants most of the day," she sighed. "I don't know what to do about it."

"What happens if you tell him to stop?" Jeanne asked.

"He will just look at me and continue as soon as I look away," she sighed. "Other parents are concerned about this too—especially Roseanne's parents. I have to tell you, I worry too—Roseanne would take off her clothes if someone told her they were her friend."

Ellen agreed that the sexual behavior of the students with cognitive disabilities needed to be permanently stopped.

Jeanne called the Association for Retarded Citizens, or ARC, to see if Robbie's parents could bring him there to get this sexual behavior stopped once and for all. She had a surprising conversation with Mrs. Lee, the director of the local parents' group. "These individuals may have a mental age similar to a five- or six-year-old," she explained. "But physically they are young adults with the same hormonal drives as other teenagers. They have strong physical feelings, but they don't have appropriate words or ways to express them."

"What do you mean, express them?" Jeanne asked. "Shouldn't they just be stopped?"

"Why do you think you have the right to make that decision?" Mrs. Lee replied.

"Well," Jeanne stammered, "because they are developmentally disabled."

Mrs. Lee patiently explained that there were ways to inform individuals with limited intellectual capacity about appropriate sexual behavior that did not preclude their right to make choices. It happened that the local ARC had received an educational grant to teach sex education to individuals with severe disabilities. Mrs. Lee was pleased to work with the school district and agreed to send someone to teach a special class on the topic of hormonal changes to the students.

Although hesitant about this revolutionary idea, Jeanne sent permission letters home with the students. A few days later Ellen called, and she was quite upset. Word about the sex class for the special education students had percolated around the district like a snowstorm and the chance of early dismissal. The teachers were incredulous. Sex education? For the retarded? What is this all about? Are they going to teach them how to do it?

"Everybody's harassing me in the teachers' room," Ellen reported in her phone call to Jeanne. "I'm not going back there ever again. They don't think these older kids should be in an elementary school and neither do I. They are so out of place in the kindergarten wing, and now with this sex thing the teachers want to make sure I am watching the kids every single minute."

Ellen's students had never bothered anybody; however, earlier that day she had gotten in trouble because Eddie went down the hall to get a drink. "I was watching him from my doorway, but the principal called me into his office and said I should never let anybody in my class out of the room alone." Eddie had been getting a drink for three years—now he was not allowed to walk down the hall alone. "I feel my students are prisoners," Ellen said.

When Jeanne met with her that afternoon, the students had gone home. It was early January and pictures of snowmen lined the halls. They all looked the same, three white balls topped with a black top hat. Even Ellen's students had produced snowmen.

In her classroom at the back of the school, Ellen pummeled her supervisor with questions about teaching sex education to students who are developmentally disabled. "William started putting his hands in his pants too," she lamented, her voice rising. "This is not what I was trained to teach. I don't have any idea how to teach this sort of thing, and I don't think I should have to."

Ellen mentioned talking to her union representative, and Jeanne sighed deeply. That would not help matters; no wonder special education wasn't appreciated in the district. Schools were supposed to teach reading and writing. When did they become responsible to do something about boys who walked around with their hands in their pants and girls willing to take theirs off?

"Tell William that he'll go blind if he doesn't stop," Jeanne suggested, but Ellen was not amused.

Back in her office, Jeanne called to ask the consultant from ARC to meet with her and help figure out how best to manage a situation like this. An appointment was arranged for later that same week. She wondered what kind of a person to expect; who would teach retarded people about sex?

Much to her relief an older lady who closely resembled Dr. Ruth Westheimer, America's favorite sex therapist of the 1980s, walked into the office. She was short with thin brown hair, glasses on a red-beaded chain, and hazel eyes that carefully absorbed Jeanne's anxiety. Mrs. Goldman took both of Jeanne's hands, and the wrinkles around her mouth turned up in a warm smile of reassurance.

Jeanne borrowed a chair from the classroom next door, and they sat with knees almost touching in the tiny office. Mrs. Goldman explained how important it was to provide specific instruction about sexual activity to individuals with intellectual disabilities. Institutions for those with developmental disabilities were built to protect them from sexual predators and bearing children. Now they were living in the community and were vulnerable. They could be easily violated by predators or just high school boys on a lark or a dare.

"It must be very specific instruction," Mrs. Goldman said. "We can't say, 'be good,' or 'don't touch.' We must show our students exactly what we mean." She had photographs of nude men and women and explained that she would use the photographs—not illustrations—that might confuse the students. She would teach the names of the parts of the body: penis, vagina, and breasts. She would teach the students that there are public and private parts of the body just like there are public and private places. We can only touch private parts of our bodies when we are in private places. She would show an erection, semen, and intercourse.

"What else are you going to say about actual sex?" Jeanne asked. "I mean, should they really be allowed to have sex?"

"I don't feel I have the right to make that decision for someone, even if the individual has a developmental disability," Mrs. Goldman replied calmly and carefully. "They are people and have the right to make decisions about their own lives. However, this program emphasizes that responsibilities come along with rights. I tell young people that they are not ready to have a girlfriend or a boyfriend until they can live independently, away from their parents. When they are ready to do that, then and only then, are they ready to have a relationship that includes sex."

"What about birth control? Do you teach them about that?"

"We teach that not having sex is the best, but I am going to show them what a condom is and how to use it."

It sounded logical and important when Mrs. Goldman explained it, and they selected dates for a twelve-week sex education program. After Mrs. Goldman left, Ellen, the instructional aide, Mrs. Blinker, and two other special education teachers from the high school crowded into the tiny office. They wanted to know if there was really going to be a sex education program.

"Yes we are having a sex education program," Jeanne stated flatly. "Ellen, you are going to observe the class along with Mrs. Blinker. You will assist Mrs. Goldman with the kids if she needs help."

"Do I have to teach it?" Ellen asked.

"No, you don't have to present the material, but you should review the lesson with the students during the week so they don't forget." Ellen's eyes glazed over and her mouth formed a tiny "O."

A curious resource center teacher had joined the little group. Jeanne wagged a finger at her, obviously only pretending to be serious. "Susan," Jeanne said, "you are not married, so you are not allowed in here. I don't want you hearing about masturbation." Everyone laughed and the tension evaporated.

The next morning Jeanne was called over to the superintendent's office for an emergency meeting. It was already a busy morning, and she regretted her new phone more and more. When she arrived, Ellen's elementary principal, Irv, was already sitting in one of the high-backed leather chairs at the superintendent's oval conference table next to his sunny office window.

Short and slight, Irv was reminiscent of an undertaker with both a great deal of concern for the dead and a sense of humor about it. He started the meeting by listing the seventeen phone calls he had received from parents regarding the mentally retarded and sex education. "These parents are afraid of the retarded kids," he said. "They think one of them might start grabbing little kids. There have been problems already in church."

He turned to Dr. Norman, the superintendent, and explained, "I have the retarded kids coming in a separate door at the back of the school, and we send them home early so the other kids and parents aren't around, but this sex education stuff has gotten everybody all riled up."

"Irv—that's illegal," Jeanne interrupted, "you can't make the special ed. kids go home early. The length of their school day is mandated." Dr. Norman calmly reminded her to stick to the topic at hand. He was a tall man with perfectly spaced features. Dignified and careful, he typically listened more than he spoke.

"Anyway," she continued to Irv's dull stare, "those students are all much too old to be in the elementary building. Eddie is seventeen and William is almost twenty-one. They should be with more age-appropriate peers." She turned to Dr. Norman, "That class should be housed in the high school."

"I don't believe this kind of student has the intelligence to benefit from being in an academic high school," he responded flatly. "We don't want to compromise our standards."

"What's the goal of an education?" Jeanne asked. "Isn't it so they can go to church, the mall, or a movie? We have to teach them how to act in the community of their peers."

"I think things like that are the parents' responsibilities, not ours, Jeanne," Dr. Norman replied. "What's this about pornography?" he asked, firmly returning to the issue at hand.

"You can't tell an individual with intellectual impairments about something—you have to show them very specifically," she replied, grateful to Mrs. Goldman for her recent education. Her palms were sweaty, and she felt attacked.

"There's a board meeting Monday night, and I want you to come and explain this," he said. "I have received several calls myself."

In a panic, Jeanne called Mrs. Goldman as soon as she got back to her office. "We can't do this," she told her. "The teachers are accusing me of teaching retarded kids to have sex. Parents are afraid the special education students will attack their children, and now I have to go talk to the board of education about using pornography."

"Ah," Mrs. Goldman said calmly. "You are relatively new in your job, but now everyone is aware of who you are and what you represent. You must fight for the rights of handicapped people to live and work in the community. Jeanne, it is very important that you consider this a great opportunity. Most of the time people don't want to hear anything about those with handicaps; now everyone is interested and they are all paying attention. Don't miss this wonderful chance to teach them something."

That was not the answer she wanted to hear. Jeanne wanted this whole thing to be over. She did not want to go to a public board of education meeting and face an interrogation.

Things have a way of going from bad to worse in a heartbeat. That afternoon, when the students in Ellen's class were heading for the bus, Angelo, a sixth-grade boy shoved Robbie in the hallway. "Ya pervert," he shouted at Robbie. "Get on the tard cart, and never come back." Ellen witnessed the whole thing, and sent Angelo to the office.

"What do you want to do about this?" Irv said when he called Jeanne. His question made her angry, and she closed her eyes in frustration. Wasn't the building principal supposed to take care of discipline? Was there one set of rules for shoving a regular kid and another set of rules for shoving a special ed. kid?

"What happens when one student hurts someone?" she asked.

"His parents have to meet with me, and he gets a one-day suspension."

"Why would this be different?"

"Okay, if that's what you want," Irv replied, but Jeanne could tell that even he thought this was different. Angelo had no personal reason to attack Robbie. He was acting out for others in the school. The standard punishment wasn't anything that would help to resolve the situation. It was just going to make everything worse. Angelo would be angry and might instigate other attacks away from Ellen's watchful eyes. Irv didn't know what to do about this situation. That's why he had called her.

"I'll come to the meeting with Angelo and his parents tomorrow morning."

"Fine," Irv said. "I'll see you first thing tomorrow."

They met at eight o'clock sharp in Irv's large office at the front of the school. Irv sat behind the stacks of papers on his desk, and Jeanne sat with Angelo and his father in a semicircle of chairs on the other side of it. Angelo had a chin that jutted right out into the room. He was compact and tapped his left foot on the floor. He resembled his father who appeared defensive and apprehensive at the same time.

Mr. Antonio said that he hoped the meeting wouldn't last long because he had to get to work. He was a plumber and would not be paid for the time he missed. He explained that Angelo's mother had passed away two years ago and that Angelo's grandmother had been helping, but she had broken her hip during the summer. She was unable to help with

Angelo anymore. "He's a good boy, but I've had a rough time lately," he said looking down at his hands. Dark circles of dirt edged his ragged fingernails.

Angelo was full of excuses. First he said that he hadn't seen Robbie. Then he said that Robbie moved too slowly and blocked the hall. He added that another kid had pushed him into Robbie when they tried to get by.

"Even if you didn't mean to shove him, why did you call him a pervert and his school bus the *tard cart*?" Jeanne asked.

"I thought that's what it's called. Everybody says that," Angelo stated flatly. He gripped the edges of his chair with his hands. "What are you picking on me for?"

"Angelo, I don't want to pick on you," she said, leaning forward to see if he would look at her. "We don't allow anybody to pick on anybody at this school."

Jeanne turned to his father. "Let's assume that this incident happened because Angleo really doesn't know Robbie," she suggested. Angelo's father nodded with interest. "I would like to have Angelo ride the school bus with Robbie for the rest of this week. The bus will pick up Angelo at your house and then pick up the rest of the kids. I think that would be a better consequence than suspending Angelo and having him stay home alone for a day and watch TV."

Mr. Antonio nodded his agreement, and Irv agreed as well. Angelo sputtered and grabbed at his father's arm as they left the room. Everyone could hear them arguing in the hall, and Jeanne assumed that Angelo would try to skip school for the rest of the week.

Irv walked Angelo to the special education bus at the close of the day. He introduced him to the kids and Carmen, the bus driver. Robbie, oblivious to the fact that Angelo had shoved him, shouted "Hello Angelo!" several times with everybody else. They were excited to have a new student on the bus.

The next morning Angelo was waiting for the bus outside of his house, Carmen reported. He got on and sat right behind her. He rode the bus back and forth every day that week. "The kids were real happy to see him," Carmen reported with a chuckle. "Everybody had to shout 'Hello Angelo' every time somebody else got on the bus."

Long after the week of bus rides in the *tard cart*, everyone in the special class waved and called to Angelo whenever they saw him. Angelo, like a movie star, would nod and wave to his adoring public with a slight smile. Robbie was particularly fascinated and always tried to get Angelo's attention. Much to his delight, Angelo often responded with "My man, Robbie," and a high five. When we know someone, we are less likely to hate them. Big, small, disabled, or brilliant, we are all more human than anything else.

The night of the board meeting featured the threat of an ice storm after midnight. Before they went into the cafeteria where the board of education held their meetings, Dr. Norman coached, "Jeanne, be brief, brief, brief! I have a long agenda tonight, and I don't want this to last until two in the morning. Whatever you have to say, cut it in half. Less is better."

Jeanne felt awkward when her turn before the board came. Following protocol, she stood facing the board members with her back to the concerned citizens who had come to the meeting. Despite the impending storm, there were plenty of people in the audience, and Jeanne sensed a great deal of attention when her name and special education came up on the agenda. Several members leaned forward in their seats and others nodded knowingly at each other. Obviously the board members had heard about the sex education issue. She was grateful and relieved that they listened carefully to what she had to say. It was not outward hostility, but curiosity.

Jeanne explained that students with intellectual disabilities needed specific instruction in order to become full participants in the community and productive members of society. Most research on sex education demonstrates that the better informed the individual, the less inappropriate sexual behavior occurs.

After Jeanne spoke, several members of the board appeared to be supportive. They not only listened but asked questions. "Are these kids capable of having, you know, sex?"

"Although they have some diminished mental capacity, physically most individuals with developmental disabilities experience the same hormonal changes that all adolescents do. Their class should be moved to the high school with students who are closer in age."

"What are the safety issues?"

"Nobody in the special class is going to touch the younger children, especially if they are taught what is appropriate touching and what is not," she explained. "I am more concerned about other students taking advantage of them."

"Shouldn't we protect them by keeping the class at the elementary school?"

"No," she replied, firm in her conviction. "I think that if our high school students got to know the kids in our special class, they would not make fun of them. Some might even get interested and be willing to assist them in the school and the community. Ignorance is what causes fear and other misunderstandings."

Jeanne left the board meeting with a new appreciation for the concerned citizens who step up to the plate and join boards of education. Several had tried to be open-minded and seemed to care about all the students—not just the athletes. She felt supported for the first time. Dr. Norman assured her that since members of the board were interested in moving the class to the high school, he would talk to the high school and find some space there for the class.

A stamp of approval from the board of education took the froth out of the talk in the teacher's room. The first session of sex education was scheduled for Tuesday afternoon beginning in late February. After each class, Mrs. Goldman stopped by to let Jeanne know how it went.

"What a wonderful group of young people. They were all attentive, and very interested in this topic," she beamed, fingering her eyeglass chain.

"How did the teachers do?" Jeanne wanted to know if they had been supportive. She was hopeful they would follow through with the lessons during the week.

"They are on board with this, Jeanne," Mrs. Goldman replied. "The teachers know all too well how carefully we must teach. They understand that this is new vocabulary, and they will reinforce it."

Several weeks into the course, Mrs. Goldman reported that things continued to go well, but she had encountered a small problem. That afternoon she showed the students a condom and let them all touch it so they would not be intimidated. "I also told them when to use it," she continued carefully, "but we hit a snag when I tried to simulate how to put one on."

She had rolled the condom down over two fingers and the boys were very attentive. "Robbie and Jeff seemed to consider this information special." Mrs. Goldman tilted her chin down to look carefully at Jeanne. "Unfortunately, that is exactly what they are going to do—they are going to put the condom on over their fingers," she said. "I could see in their eyes." Mrs. Goldman paused and leaned forward, "I am going to have to use a dildo."

"You're kidding!" Dr. Norman said when Jeanne called to inform him about this development. She also wanted to make sure she had his permission. "Hey, what the heck—if she needs to demonstrate, then do it." Jeanne could hear him chuckle as he put down the phone. She knew that special education had indeed won this little skirmish when nobody said a thing about the dildo in the classroom.

The sex education program gave Ellen a simple way to inform students about sexual topics—in language that they could understand. There are public and private rooms. The classroom is a public room; the bathroom is private. There are public and private parts of the body. Our shoulders are public, breasts are private. We can only touch public parts of our own body while we are in a public place like the classroom, the hallway, and the lunchroom. We only touch public parts of another person's body like the hands and the shoulders. The bedroom is a private place and we can touch private parts of our body there. No one but a doctor can touch private parts of our body.

When Eddie put his hands in his pants, Ellen firmly reminded him that he was in a public place, and he stopped immediately. Eventually she just needed to point to a picture of public places, and he would nod and stop. Knowing that there was a private place seemed to help him.

Jeanne teased Ellen about it when she shared this success. "It's a good thing you stopped him, Ellen," she quipped. "He could'a gone blind at the rate he was going."

Robbie's mother and several other parents called in support of moving the special class to the high school. "My son is almost nineteen," she said. "He should not be in the elementary school." Irv also agreed that the class should be moved to the high school.

The high school principal was opposed to the idea. "We don't have any room up here," he protested loudly when it was broached with him. "If you and your friends on the board think that I'm going to move a hundred and twenty-five math students so you can have an entire classroom for eight retarded kids—you are nuts," he sputtered. "That's a ridiculous idea. Retarded kids shouldn't be in a high school. We don't teach the days of the week up here!"

That spring, during the break, the class did move. The band was told to store their instruments in the band room instead of a basement classroom. The band director was upset because the basement room had a door to the parking lot and they could easily take the instruments off the bus and store them. Once the superintendent ordered him to find a room for the class, Bruce had insisted on the basement classroom because he thought the special class should come into the building through the back door. He plainly didn't want the kids with disabilities coming into the front of the building.

The instruments were moved out of the basement room and some old desks and tables were moved in. The new special education classroom had large windows that opened onto the parking lot and was cooler than the rest of the building in the hot months of May and June.

A high school feels categorically different from elementary schools and middle schools. High schools pulsate, they practically throb. You can pick up the energy in the parking lot. It's not the staff—it's the students. They are excited and exciting. Put a group of fourteen- to eighteen-year-olds together and you have an event that is best described as sexual tension. It is all mostly nuance that pulses with the sheer joy young people experience in human contact. It is contagious. High school teachers catch it. There are funny jokes in the teachers' room and innuendos passed around meetings.

You will never encounter this in an elementary school where the main things passed around are recipes for brownies and shepherd's pie. Middle school teachers rarely talk to each other unless you are in the correct group of friends. One group eats in the teachers' room, some meet in one another's classroom and talk about those who are eating in the lunchroom. What does it mean? Are kids contagious? The best charades players are elementary school teachers—they can sound out anything and communicate well with body language. Don't tell them a raunchy joke—they won't get it. Both Ellen and her students had a big adjustment to make!

Ellen decided to have an open house at the end of the first week so the high school teachers could meet her special education students. She sent everyone an invitation for coffee and doughnuts. Each morning that week, Ellen and her students role-played greeting someone at the door and offering them a cup of coffee and a doughnut.

On the day of the open house, the students helped to put a red table-cloth on the table and measure the coffee. One by one the five other special education teachers at the high school came down to say hello. Not one single person from any other department dropped by. Bruce did not come. Perhaps he was too busy picking up papers in the hall. About eleven o'clock, Larry, one of the assistant principals, stood uneasily by the door. His arms were firmly crossed over a belly that rose over the top of his khaki pants.

Oblivious to his grim mouth and stare, Ellen told Becky to greet him. She went over to the door, and since he didn't move or say anything, she stared at him with an open mouth. Ellen tapped her shoulder and whispered, "Becky, what do you say at the door?"

"Hello?" Becky asked, searching Ellen's face for the answer. Larry shifted to the other foot as if this was exactly what he expected.

"Hi Larry, thanks for coming," Ellen smiled cheerfully, carefully ignoring his attitude. "Come on in, don't be shy!" She ushered him into the room while she motioned for Becky to follow her. Larry was clearly uncomfortable, but Ellen was not finished with him for sticking his big stomach into her room. "Hey Becky," she said. "Mr. Larry likes candy." She gestured over to the red tablecloth and a bowl of shining Hershey's kisses on the table. "Give him some kisses."

Becky's eyes got big and her lips closed together into one big happy smile, but she didn't go over to the table. She reached up and put both hands around Larry's neck. Before anyone knew what was happening, she pulled his head down and kissed him right on the lips.

"I love you," she said. Larry sputtered and staggered backward as though he'd been doused with ice water.

"Becky!" Ellen shouted with her palms next to her face, feigning horror. "I meant candy kisses—not real kisses. Tell Mr. Larry you're sorry."

Becky looked uncertainly at her teacher, then she hung her head. "Sorry—no touching," she said motionless and miserable. Larry waved his hand and mumbled that everything was okay with him. The rest of the students went over to console Becky who regarded Larry out of the corner of her eye.

"Larry, why don't you take a plate of doughnuts up to the main of-fice?" Ellen said, ignoring the wailing. "We have a lot of leftovers." She turned, glared at the little pity party, and stopped it with a look. "Rob-bie," she directed firmly, "Pour Mr. Larry a cup of coffee." Larry left with a Styrofoam cup of coffee and a paper plate piled high with sugary doughnuts and chocolate kisses.

It was late and obviously no other faculty members would be coming down to welcome the new class when Jeanne arrived to see how the day had gone. Ellen told the students they could take a paper plate and pick out one doughnut to put on it. "Pay attention to what you are doing," she warned. "If you drop it, you have to throw it away. We do not eat things that fall on the floor." Everyone carefully walked over to the wooden table at the back of the classroom where they ate in silence with Mrs. Blinker, the classroom aide.

"Larry looked like a deer in headlights," Ellen quipped as she sur-veyed the platters of leftover doughnuts. "What a typical administrator!"

"Hey, what about me? Am I a typical administrator?" Jeanne asked. Ellen didn't offer any support for her administrative efforts, and Jeanne decided not to pursue it.

"Jeanne," Ellen laughed, "he was afraid of the kids! What a hoot." Ellen talked about what could be done to better integrate her students into high school activities.

"Maybe seeing everybody at once is overwhelming," Jeanne sug-gested. All together they looked worse than they did individually. You couldn't help but think about us and them. They are stupid; we are smart. They are dirty; we are clean.

"We need to integrate one student at a time," Ellen suggested. "How about sending Becky up to get the mail from the main office? I don't think they will tell us she can't do that." Teachers often sent a student to the main office to pick up their mail. The students were not allowed in the back; however they stopped at the chest high counter and asked one of the secretaries if the teacher had any mail. Someone would retrieve it from the mailboxes at the rear of the office and hand it to the student. Some students were even allowed behind the counter to retrieve the mail.

"Send Becky with Mrs. Blinker for a few days until she can find the office and ask for the mail on her own," Jeanne suggested.

Mrs. Blinker was hesitant at first; however, she agreed, and it was decided that on Monday morning Becky would follow Mrs. Blinker up to the office. What could anyone say? Other students did this every day. It was unlikely that anyone would forbid a specific student from coming into the office. Besides, Becky would have an adult with her.

Monday morning, Jeanne made sure she was standing in the main office at the precise time Ellen sent Becky up to get her mail. The office buzzed with parents reporting sick students, the whir of the Xerox machine in its sunny room, and a line of students waiting in the metal and orange plastic chairs for Larry to give them a late pass to class.

As soon as Becky followed Mrs. Blinker into the room, Elaine, the head secretary, gasped and all went silent. Three secretaries and the office assistant sat and gaped openly at Becky as though she was a stray dog. Jeanne was furious and wanted to shout, "Guess what? She's not contagious!" Becky kept her eyes down and her hands dangled at her sides while Mrs. Blinker got the daily teachers' bulletin and some notices from Ellen's mailbox. Elaine picked up a ringing phone but asked the caller to please hold as if she needed to make sure that Becky was going to leave the room and go back downstairs where she belonged.

Mrs. Blinker glanced back uneasily as she left to see if Becky was behind her. Becky slowly turned and followed her, eyes on the floor. Just in the doorframe, she suddenly tossed her head back toward the silent secretaries and a big smile emerged. She is actually pretty when she smiles, Jeanne realized. Leaning slightly back into the room, Becky dramatically flipped her marvelous mane of chestnut curls and said quite distinctly, "Au revoir!" She skipped on down the hall after Mrs. Blinker and was gone. After a moment of confused silence, the office erupted—in laughter.

"Who was that? What a cute girl—and French! She speaks French?"

Jeanne was as stunned as everyone else. She wanted to confirm what she thought she heard Becky say. "Au revoir?"

"Yes, that's what she said," Elaine smiled.

"That was Becky," Jeanne explained. "She's in the special education class we just brought up from the elementary school."

"Well, how sweet," said Elaine. "At first I didn't know what to think," she spoke for everyone. "But she was polite as can be. They don't hurt anybody, do they?"

Jeanne explained that the students with developmental disabilities were all very sweet-natured. "Some of the kids don't speak clearly; however, if you listen closely, you'll probably be able to understand them." Larry came out of his office to see what all the noise was about and stood there blinking slowly. Yes, a deer in headlights.

On the day after the students left for the summer, Bruce decided to order a computer for the self-contained classroom for children with developmental disabilities. He explained that he had a little money left over in his budget. At the end of the fiscal year on June 30 any money left in school accounts is swept into a surplus account controlled by the superintendent. "I'd rather spend it on our kids than let the superintendent have it and give it to another school," Bruce explained. Somehow even he had accepted the special class and the special students.

ESSENTIAL UNDERSTANDINGS

- When schools opened special classes for students with severe disabilities in the early 1980s, the first issue that arose was what to teach. The curriculum needed to be expanded to include aspects of community life.
- As students aged, they often remained in elementary schools due to perceptions that since they did not mature intellectually, they did not mature physically. Individuals with developmental disabilities experience the same hormonal changes that all adolescents do.
- Parents and teachers were confronted with developmental issues such as sexual drives and menstruation they were not prepared to address. Once individuals with intellectual disabilities (ID) began to live in the community, they were prey to sexual abuse.
- Forward-thinking agencies such as the Association for Retarded Citizens (ARC), developed curriculum around sexual issues for teachers and parents.
- Conceptualizing ideas into concrete terms proved useful. The concept of public and private people and places was understandable to most students with ID.
- This positive outcome was primarily due to the support of the members of the board of education. The IDEA was written due to the efforts of parents, and advocacy efforts remain important.

THREE

Attention!

An Egyptian papyrus dated 1552 describes 700 different opium mixtures including one for calming bothersome children.

It is always a surprise to teachers when a parent disagrees with them and insists their child is disabled. Anthony seemed like an active, normally developing, six–year-old to his teacher who had over twelve years of experience with first graders.

His mother said he didn't listen to her, lost his jackets, toys, and books, was always running around, and never played quietly. She knew these were characteristics of attention deficit hyperactivity disorder, or ADHD. The school diagnostic team and his teacher saw Anthony as a typical little boy who loved to run and jump and didn't like sitting in a seat writing letters. His mother felt he had ADHD and fought to have him classified as disabled.

Parental demands for special education services are distressing to school administrators. They can often barely meet the substantial needs of children with severe disabilities and resent parents who demand extensive services for children with minimal problems.

The parents of children with developmental disabilities bravely face the rest of their lives with a dependent person. Services such as respite care or group homes are scarce, with long waiting lists. Frequently families have to wait until one parent dies and the other is disabled for the situation to be considered an emergency. Only then can their adult child with a developmental disability be moved to a group home.

Public schools have limited services to offer their most needy students since the Individuals with Disabilities Education Act (IDEA) has never been fully funded. The federal government supplies only a few hundred dollars a year per student. After a six-and-a-half hour school day, families are on their own. Even these services end when a child turns twenty-one. Then entitlement under the IDEA is over and the waiting lists begin.

Some parents of typically developing children want to have them classified under the IDEA so they would be eligible for special classes, additional time on the SAT, door-to-door transportation, and other advantages. There were loopholes in the special education law big enough for savvy lawyers to get whatever parents wanted. Attorneys bragged that the law was so ambiguous they could win any case. Rather than risk the cost of litigation, school districts may even agree to parental demands.

In one New Jersey case, a litigious parent claimed his daughter was handicapped and needed home instruction due to an undisclosed illness. Her condition did not impact her ability to excel academically, participate on sport teams, or participate in other after-school activities. The school multidisciplinary team acquiesced to the pressure and classified her. Based on the individual tutoring in all of her advanced placement courses, she earned all A's and her grade point average made her the school valedictorian.

Teachers and administrators, including the superintendent, denied her eligibility and said that a student with individual tutors did not earn the same grades as general education students in large classes. A judge ruled that because the district had determined that this student was handicapped, this was illegal discrimination. His ruling meant that the special education student was indeed the valedictorian.

The weather during the last week of school was hot and sticky. The thermometer seemed stuck at over eighty-five degrees. Sweaty t-shirts stuck to bodies; sweaty fingers stuck to paper. No one suspected what else would get stuck before the school year was over. That spring had been especially stressful for the principal and the director of special services. A parent at the elementary school insisted that her six-year-old son, Anthony, had ADHD. When the school's diagnostic team did not agree, she threatened legal action.

Now the ground was soggy, and a steaming mist hung over the soccer field behind the school. It was so wet that a flock of sea gulls had settled in to squawk about the score. It was too humid for the water to evaporate, too hot to move. It had been a difficult year and everyone was tired by the time the sultry days of June rolled around. Teachers gasped for breath and knew that it was time for the school year to end. There was no longer any point in continuing. They had done enough, and so had the sweaty little people they call students.

The teachers were anxious about their final recommendations. Who will pass? Who will be kept back? Tempers flared, tension mounted, and everyone felt overwhelmed by it all. Then the heat came. The buildings trapped the hot air like the lid on a pot. The sun beat down on flat black roofs and cooked the occupants. First, the sunny south wing became unbearable, and then there was no escape except in the air-conditioned teachers' room or the principal's office.

The parent teacher association (PTA) mothers bought fans from the remainder of their budget. They blew hot air around the classrooms and were so noisy that teachers could only stare at the listless students. Four hundred and eighteen hot sweaty children ran in from the playground after lunch. That alone raised the temperature in the building another seven degrees. No one said, "Hasn't this year gone by quickly!" in the teachers' room anymore.

That last hot Monday afternoon, a flatbed truck loaded with shingles for the new school roof lumbered down the one way circular drive at the side of the building. The driver pulled up next to the door by the special education classrooms. The director of special services happened to see him drive up on her way to visit a teacher, and went out to investigate.

"You can't park here," she told him in her best administrative voice. "Seven special education buses are coming to pick up children in about forty minutes. Some of the children are in wheelchairs and you can't block this entrance to the school with your truck."

The driver looked up and down the street. There was no other place to put the truck other than the main entrance and he had already been told not to park there. Angrily he eased the truck back around the curved driveway. Then he stopped, shifted gears, and turned left over the sidewalk and down onto the soccer field. The sixteen wheeler easily rolled down the grassy hill. However; as soon as the full length of the truck leveled out, the wheels began to sink and were quickly sucked up to the axles by the mud in the sodden soccer field. The seagulls scattered. Score!

Perhaps the driver was perceptually impaired and has attention deficit disorder (ADD), the director thought. Obviously he had not considered why a flock of seagulls were sitting on a grassy field before he drove a fully loaded truck onto it. Poor impulse control and frequent accidents are some of the things cited in the diagnosis of children with ADD; however, there was no clear definition and sometimes the diagnosis was a palliative label for stupid behavior.

Back in the dim hallway, Jeanne Carter, the director, wondered if she should report the sunken truck to the building principal, but made an administrative decision to stay out of this mess. The building principal is responsible for building maintenance and would not appreciate a reminder about a serious problem from a director of special services.

Relationships were always tenuous since so many extraordinary adjustments were needed for the children with special needs. They needed a special schedule, different books, a room for a small class in a full building. She decided to continue with her plan to check on how one of the special education teachers, Debbie, was doing. Debbie had a difficult class that included Anthony, the little boy diagnosed with ADHD basically due to his mother's threats of a lawsuit.

There was no doubt that Anthony was an active boy. He wandered around the classroom and bounced when he sat in his seat. His papers were messy, and his backpack often contained old lunches and crumpled notices. He was cute and mischievous. He took too much glue and got it all over his pants; he raced around the room during indoor recess playing airplane. He had an angelic face framed by curls the pale color of moonlight, and an "O" for a mouth. It was hard to take misbehavior seriously, when the perpetrator looks like cupid. Anthony had perfected the angelic look.

If Anthony had a disability, to the teachers, it was childhood. In kindergarten he went to the bathroom with Richard Parsley and had water fights. In first grade, he was the first one out of his seat and the last one in from recess. As soon as his teacher announced a spelling test, he had to go to the bathroom or the nurse. He jiggled in his seat and shouted out the correct answers to every question. If a truck rumbled by or students laughed while they passed the classroom in the hall, he would get up and go and look out the window or door.

Anthony's favorite subject was gym and his worst was penmanship. He brought little robots to school and created a miniature world inside his desk. His spelling papers were crumpled up and used to make volcanoes. His teacher thought he needed clear limits and structure. She felt that six-year-old children needed more recess time, but that was no longer allowed due to all the emphasis on test preparation. His mother thought he needed to be in small classes where he would receive extra attention. His father was a lawyer.

Anthony's mother complained in September that he was not reading. His first-grade teacher reassured her that Anthony was just not interested in books like many other first-grade boys. She explained that most of the children in her class only knew a few sight words when school started. Anthony knew all his letters and could count to one hundred. He had good beginning first-grade skills.

However, his mother insisted something was wrong, so the teacher made a referral to the weekly Pupil Assistance Team meeting. This committee is composed of the school nurse, the principal, the social worker, the school psychologist, and teachers from each grade. They meet each week to discuss any students of concern and make a plan of action.

The committee members agreed with Anthony's teacher that nothing was fundamentally wrong with him. They noted that his parents both worked so he was dropped off at school at seven in the morning and also went to after-care. He was picked up about 5:30 p.m. They felt the long day might explain some of his restlessness. They also noted that he had an August birthdate and was the youngest child in the first grade.

Many of the boys in his class had been held out of school for an extra year and were almost eight while Anthony was barely six. They suggested he have plenty of opportunities to move including frequent breaks and trips around the school. His teacher agreed and decided to include movement breaks more frequently during her class. They sang the Hokey Pokey song and began with large movements and ended with small controlled movements and whispered the words.

In October, when Anthony did not make the top reading group, but was placed in the middle group, his mother went ballistic. She called the superintendent of schools, the county office, and the State Department of Education.

"They have refused to do an evaluation of my child. He is ADHD and they are refusing to see his handicap," she insisted. Any parent has a right to request an evaluation under the IDEA. The request must be in writing and the district must respond with a meeting. Most requests for evaluations come from classroom teachers who see the range of children in their classes. They are usually quite accurate in determining who needs special education services.

Letters on heavy paper from Brown and Sadwaite began to arrive in the office of special services. They requested a full evaluation of Anthony. When a parent requests an evaluation to determine eligibility for special education services, the multidisciplinary team (MDT) usually composed of an administrator, a psychologist, the child's teacher, a special education teacher, and the parent meet to decide what if any, evaluations are necessary.

It is typical practice for a MDT to conduct a full evaluation even if they feel that the student is not handicapped. The evaluations can provide test evidence to present to the parents that will either support the team's conclusion or reveal a disability. A team is not required by the IDEA to evaluate the student unless there is some indication that the child may have a disability; however, even when none is suspected, most diagnostic teams will evaluate the child when parents insist, because symptoms may be subtle.

The school psychologist tested Anthony. Anthony was a model student during every aspect of his psychological testing. His WISQ IQ scores came out at or above age expectancy on all of the subtests. He sat perfectly still when Dr. Kinder observed him in the classroom.

Nancy, the learning disability teacher consultant, gave Anthony the Woodcock Johnson test of achievement. He had to get a drink of water and go off to the bathroom five times in one hour. He fidgeted and wiggled and ended up with his little feet in the air waving at her from upside down. Nancy supposed the big chairs were uncomfortable for a little guy. This was a kid who wanted to be comfortable, she remarked. He was so adorable Nancy wanted to take him home. Her testing revealed that when he was not interested in the task, his performance fell, but he loved other parts of the testing and had scores that were well-above expectations for his age.

Both the learning disabilities consultant and his teacher saw the same things in his first-grade class. If he liked the project, he was on task, and was often the first with his hand up. If he was not interested, he looked around the room for something else to do. He chewed his t-shirt, stabbed erasers, and rolled pencils on the floor and despite this, knew the correct answers to questions the teacher asked. Unfortunately, he usually shouted out the answer without raising his hand.

The testing indicated only one area of weakness—fine motor skills. Anthony was a ball player; he could catch and throw well, but he did not like to write and he didn't care if he stayed within the lines. It didn't seem to the MDT that this young man had any severe deficits. The IDEA is not a preventative law; children are either handicapped or they are not.

Diagnostic problems are compounded when the suspected disability is ADD, attention deficit disorder, or ADHD, attention deficit disorder with hyperactivity. This disability has proven difficult to define. The Diagnostic and Statistical Manual (DSM) of the American Psychiatric Association had listed ADD with a checklist so vague that almost any active little boy could be diagnosed with ADD. "What constitutes a fidget?" experts asked. ADHD is a disability with no unique physical characteristics and no psychological or physiological tests are available.

Even without any tests, in the United States, ADHD is the most frequently diagnosed disorder in children. Most children fidget, have difficulty remaining seated and playing quietly for long periods. They frequently don't listen and interrupt; yet these behaviors are used to diagnose attention deficit hyperactivity disorder.

The characteristics of ADHD include:

- Makes careless mistakes;
- Does not seem to listen;
- Fails to finish school work or chores;
- Avoids tasks that require mental effort;
- Is often easily distracted;
- Has trouble waiting his or her turn;
- Interrupts.

Prior to 1990, The Council for Exceptional Children challenged the assumptions defining this classification and opposed efforts to make it a new disability label in the IDEA. The reauthorization of the IDEA in 1990 included it as a condition under the category of "Other Health Impaired." Despite the doubts many professionals expressed, anxious parents all over the country seeking a reason for their children's behavior, sought a diagnosis of ADD.

The social worker made several appointments to visit and gather a health and developmental history. Anthony's mother was unable to keep two of the appointments and forgot the third one entirely. "I'm so very sorry, dear," she said. "I've been so busy at work." During a telephone interview, she shared her high aspirations for Anthony. She wanted him to attend an Ivy League college like his father and become a lawyer. She felt that his undiagnosed handicap was the reason he didn't like to do homework. She sent a letter from her pediatrician stating that Anthony had ADHD.

The MDT discussed Anthony on and off all December. A diagnostic team has ninety days from the initial request to the final resolution. The psychologist reviewed his psychological testing and said Anthony did not meet any criteria to be classified as eligible for special education services. The learning disability teacher consultant felt he was an at-risk student who had the potential for problems. Everyone struggled with possible unintended consequences of calling a child handicapped who was functioning at average academic levels, but had the potential to be above average. Is that a handicap?

"Well, if we tell his mother he has a disability, he certainly will have trouble later," the psychologist argued.

"This mother needs help," added the social worker. "She is frustrated and overwhelmed by Anthony. I would like to include her in my parenting groups, but she does not get back from work until quite late."

"When parents are concerned about an active child, we stick a label on the kid and pump them full of drugs." The psychologist argued, concerned that the next step for Anthony was Ritalin.

Anthony's mother, like many parents, wanted to get everything she could for her son. It was not her fault that the special education law was vague and poorly written. It did not define handicap and left open the idea that a child doing average work but having the potential for above average work should be placed in special education where he would be helped.

It seemed that many parents were comforted when they were told their child had ADHD, instead of being someone who got into trouble at school and had trouble reading. A diagnosis of attention deficit hyperactivity disorder might give relief from the anxiety. "It is not your fault," the popular magazines reassured troubled parents, "ADHD is a medical condition."

The school district's attorney advised the team that if the school district went to court, and the parents prevailed on the case, the district would be liable for all of the legal fees. That could run into thousands of dollars. He did not advise taking a case like this to court.

Anthony had to be labeled impaired in some way in order to receive any special education services. ADHD is not one of the federally determined classifications that qualify a child as having a disability. The MDT decided to discuss classifying Anthony as Other Health Impaired with his parents. It is the disability category that can be used for children with ADHD.

"Other Health Impaired" corresponds to "Chronically Ill" and is defined as a disability characterized by having limited strength, vitality, or alertness, including a heightened alertness with respect to the educational environment, due to chronic or acute health problems, such as attention deficit disorder or attention deficit hyperactivity disorder, a heart condition, tuberculosis, rheumatic fever, nephritis, asthma, sickle cell anemia, hemophilia, epilepsy, lead poisoning, leukemia, diabetes, or any other medical condition, such as Tourette syndrome, that adversely affects a student's educational performance.

The MDT would suggest some occupational therapy for his fine motor issues, and work with the teachers and his parents to find ways to keep this energetic little boy interested in school.

During the individual educational plan (IEP) meeting, Anthony's father sat quietly and listened carefully. When the team brought up the recommendation to classify Anthony "Other Health Impaired," he remarked, "I'm glad you didn't have this when I was in school. I was just like my son. I don't think I would have become a lawyer if you had told me I had a disability."

Anthony's mother was so upset that the school personnel did not identify her son's handicap until she threatened to sue, that she had little confidence in the school's programs or personnel. She did not believe the testing and she wanted a second opinion. When a parent feels the school district's testing is inadequate, they have a right to request a second opinion paid for by the school district. Anthony's second opinion cost over three thousand dollars. District budgets do not have slush funds; money for unexpected events must come from another fund. Money budgeted for material was used to pay for it.

Private evaluators at a children's hospital conducted the evaluations. The children's specialized hospital diagnostic report consisted of twenty pages of testing results. They were consistent with the school district's findings. The teachers who worked with him day after day were right in the first place. Anthony had above average ability and his academic performance was average or above. He did demonstrate some fine motor delay. The neurologist did not see any "soft" signs of disorder.

The private diagnostic team recommended individual occupational therapy sessions three times a week, physical therapy twice a week, and two hours each day of special education instruction. They included over one hundred and fifty goals and objectives and recommended that Anthony be given a portable computer since he had problems with handwriting.

Do private evaluators even consider what a six-year-old boy was going to do with a laptop computer, or how disruptive all of these services would be to his school day? Would a three thousand dollar piece of equipment end up on the floor, or covered with chocolate milk? Even the teachers in the school didn't have laptop computers. There was a computer with a special keyboard called Intellikeys that would benefit the students in the self-contained class for students with developmental disabilities at the high school. Anthony's laptop would need to be purchased from those special funds and the self-contained class would have to wait another year.

During a telephone conference to review the hospital's report, the director of special services questioned why their recommendations were so extensive despite the minimal areas of weakness the testing revealed.

"Oh, we like to give the parents our recommendations for best practice," she was told. "We are not concerned here about costs. Under the IDEA schools have to provide whatever services are recommended," she said, alluding to the threatened lawsuit. A negative attitude toward a school system she had never even seen permeated the conversation.

The MDT of the psychologist, social worker, learning consultant, and the general and special education teacher met five more times with Anthony's mother at her request to go over the goals and objectives of Anthony's IEP. Each meeting required two substitute teachers be hired and the coordination of six different schedules.

Anthony's mother came to the last meeting with an advocate from CHADD or the Children and Adults with Attention Deficit Hyperactivity Disorder resource center, a parent advocacy association. The advocate convinced her to accept the special education program offered for her son. He would have the maximum legal limit of two hours a day in the resource center, occupational therapy two times a week, and adaptive physical education twice a week.

Anthony's mother would not compromise on the personal laptop computer for her son. When questioned about this, the district's attorney insisted that one be provided for this child to satisfy the parents and get them to settle the dispute. The little bit of money the district got from the federal government for special education students would be spent on a child who barely qualified. The IDEA has never been funded at anywhere near the 40 percent originally promised when the law was passed, Schools typically get around four hundred dollars for each classified student—nowhere near the additional cost to provide the additional services the law required. Most of the cost is paid by the local taxpayers.

Although she dropped the lawsuit and signed the IEP, Anthony's mother remained convinced that the school had willfully ignored her son's special needs. Anthony's behavior got worse as he was pulled out of first grade several times a day for all the special education therapies. He seemed to spend more time in the hall going to special classes than he did learning.

His special education teacher, Debbie, talked to his mother many times that spring to explain what Anthony did during her class and what action she took with him.

"He threw his pencil at Sherman,"

"He is hyperactive," was the response.

"Yes, but we can't allow him to throw things in the classroom."

"It says in his IEP that he is to have frequent breaks. Are you doing that?"

"Yes, he now has two desks and can move between them whenever he wants to move."

"Pencils frustrate my son, he is handicapped; he gets anxious when he has to use a pencil. Why can't he use the computer?"

"Anthony does not know how to type and he doesn't want to use the laptop because I won't let him play computer games during class. I use it as a reward if he completes his work."

"My son has poor fine motor control, that's why he doesn't like the computer."

Debbie was discouraged and frustrated. She had an excellent relationship with Anthony, whom she adored and who usually tried to please her. However, the better he liked his teacher, the more attention he wanted. He disliked sharing her with any of the other students and grew less and less willing to work on anything independently. He wanted his teacher right beside him, and he got more and more skillful at avoiding independent work. He was learning how to be helpless.

Anthony never seemed to stop moving, tapping his pencil, throwing his desk top up and rummaging around inside. He made fish faces and stuck his foot into the aisles. Then, during the first week in April he turned over a new leaf. He had eagerly looked up every single word from the vocabulary list in the dictionary. Later that week his first-grade teacher discovered that he had written "FUCK" and "SUCK" in the margins of each page. Debbie noted that these words were clearly written and showed improvement in his handwriting.

When Debbie met with Anthony's mother about this, she claimed that the school was insensitive and did not understand his special needs. He needed to be challenged. The vocabulary words were too simple, and he was expressing his boredom. He was turned off because of all the abuse he had suffered at the hands of teachers before his attention deficit disorder had been properly diagnosed and she made the school system aware of his problems. He simply could not help it and we needed to create a program for him that would meet his special needs. She would not pay for the damage to the book. Anthony's mother presented Debbie with several articles on children with attention deficit disorder.

Debbie wondered if Anthony had become more of a handful precisely because he had been placed in special education where his skills were much better than the other children. She wondered if labeling him as disabled had convinced him that he really could not control his behavior and needed help. There is a name for this, it is called *learned helplessness* but it didn't matter now; it was hot and time for summer vacation.

After she watched the truck sink into the mud, Jeanne continued her visit to see how things were progressing with Anthony. She stood outside the classroom door of the special education resource center. The overhead lights were turned off. Floor fans roared their displeasure. Debbie saw Jeanne standing by the open door and walked slowly over.

She was one of those individuals who always looked perfect. Her hair was flawlessly coiffed, her clothes impeccable, her nails beautifully manicured. Today, however, even Debbie was uncomfortable. One of her gold earrings perched at an odd angle. "This is the worst," she moaned. "I can't believe we still have four more days of school. What do they think we are teaching when it is hot like this?"

"I know," Jeanne murmured in sympathy.

"Well, the kids are hot too. They can't concentrate."

"I'll bet," she replied, nodding.

"I bought everyone a can of soda," Debbie sighed. "They can drink that to cool off a little."

As they chatted in the doorway, the classroom was dim and quiet. Even Anthony seemed in a stupor from the heat. It was not clear how well the remediation of Anthony's ADHD had succeeded, but the district had managed to get through the year without having to go to court. Perhaps that was success with this family. Everyone remained hopeful that they would eventually be able to develop a trusting relationship with Anthony's parents.

Suddenly there was muffled laughter in the classroom and Debbie wearily gave a "what now?" look. Once inside she gasped then walked quickly back over to the door and grabbed the interschool phone. She connected to the school secretary, Joyce. She clicked furiously at the receiver and hissed, "You will not believe what this child has done!" Inside the classroom, the children were all gathered around Anthony's desk.

"He sucked too hard on the soda can after it was empty and his lips went right into the opening. Now he can't get them out!" Debbie hissed, her eyes bugging out of her sweaty forehead. Sure enough, there was an orange soda can snugly attached to Anthony's face right under his sunburned little nose.

"How did he do that?" his teacher asked the other students, mystified, and still clicking the phone furiously. She muttered, "How does Anthony do anything," under her breath.

Anthony might have thought his dilemma was funny at first, but he soon realized that his teacher had no magical remedy to get his lips out of the can. This was serious—if sucking your lips inside a can be considered serious.

"Joyce," Debbie said to the school secretary, who had finally picked up. "I'm sending Anthony down to the office." She paused for a moment to consider, then added, "He has a soda can stuck on his lips."

She replaced the receiver with a firm click and returned to Anthony. She spoke calmly and reassuringly into his ear, and he nodded and slunk from his chair toward the door. The little circle of excited children drew back.

"Dr. Carter will take you down to the office," she told him not unkindly. There was no need for a negative comment; the soda can was punishment enough.

Anthony walked slowly and miserably down the long hallway to the principal's office with the can dangling from his face. Children stopped on their way to the bathroom, and teachers stared from classroom doors. No one said anything, at least not until they had stared at the poor child for as long as they possibly could, and he was out of earshot.

Jeanne followed, slightly behind the culprit. She wished she had stayed in her nice air-conditioned office that afternoon and administered something. Now there was no escape; she was going to have to deal with this situation. It was hot and she didn't know what to do when kids sucked their lips inside soda cans. Every day brought new and different challenges in the special education department but she had never seen anything like this.

The inevitable telephone call to Anthony's mother filled her with dread. It was certain that she would be furious. Would the district end up in court after all? The parents' attorney would be relentless in a situation like this in court.

"And so," he would snarl looking over the tops of his glasses. "You were chatting with the teacher while the students were unsupervised in the classroom?"

"Well yes," she would have to sputter.

"And the unsupervised students were drinking soda?"

"Yes."

"But, you just told me this was a reading class. Why were special education students drinking soda instead of the reading instruction mandated in the IEP?"

"Well it was hot."

"I have here a letter from the PTA regarding the fans they purchased for the classrooms, your honor," he would say. "Many children with special needs are sensitive to heat. The school district should be ordered to conduct classes for these children in air-conditioned rooms where learning can take place."

He would be relentless, "I have here the child's IEP, which had to be drawn up by the Children's Hospital since the school district failed to identify the child's handicap. The goals and objectives are clearly spelled out, and they do not mention 'soda drinking.' I submit that this placement is not meeting the child's educational needs."

A private school placement would cost the district at least forty thousand dollars or more plus transportation. Jeanne feared that a teacher would have to be let go.

As they rounded the last corner before the main office in the front of the building, men's voices echoed through the deserted hallway. Two of the roofers were shouting at each other, using language that was not at all suitable for a school building.

"Now what the f*** are we gonna do? Just tell me that?" the enraged construction supervisor was shouting at the truck driver.

"How was I supposed to know the stupid field was a f***ing swamp."

"It's been raining for the past week."

"So, it stopped."

"Yeah and we're ###****** stopped because the truck is up to her knees in mud."

Jeanne took Anthony's hand, concerned that he might be frightened. On the contrary, he was enjoying this glimpse into the world of men immensely. Now that's distractible, she thought, wondering how anyone could forget they had a can stuck on their face.

Anthony began to cry when they turned the corner in front of the principal's office. A large tear was hanging on the end of his nose. It fell off on the can and made a plunking sound.

The doorknob felt hot and sticky but once the door was opened a rush of cooled air greeted the visitors. Joyce must have seen Anthony through the glass windows. She had her head on her typewriter and her shoulders were shaking. The other secretaries were trying to hide their amusement as well. The principal's office door was closed. He was on the telephone, but after peering out to see who was knocking, he motioned the director inside. She quickly closed the door behind her, because he was shouting at the superintendent.

"Paul," he fulminated, "when you go for the lowest bid you get stuff like this. Now what am I going to do about the soccer field? Even when they get the truck out it will be totally ripped up. I've got four hundred parents coming to our graduation at the end of the week and a truck for a centerpiece."

"Can you believe this," he said as he hung up the phone. "How am I gonna get that truck outta here? What an idiot driver!"

Jeanne quickly changed the subject. "I brought Anthony down because he's having a little bit of a problem." The principal rested his chin on his hand and his eyes glazed over. He was counting the years until Anthony went on to bigger and better things like middle school. "You had better take a look at him before you go out there," she suggested.

He looked perplexed, but long years with four hundred children had made him continually curious. He peered through the glass at Anthony in the outer office and burst out laughing. "How could this happen?" He said between guffaws.

"He must have sucked so hard, he sucked his lips inside the opening of the can."

"I can't believe this!"

A sharp rap on the door window interrupted the brief moment of sanity. It was the school nurse. She was meticulous, hypercritical, and a tiger mother when it came to the needs of her charges. She was action oriented and not of the "let's wait and see what happens" persuasion.

"We've got an emergency here," she said in her high-pitched finger-pointing voice.

"I know," the principal said pulling his mouth together with a great deal of effort. "I am reviewing the situation."

"I think you should call an ambulance and take this child to the emergency room," she demanded, staring directly at him for emphasis.

"Well, I think we could try something here first before we start over-doing this," he started to say, but she was already gone. She herded Anthony into her little office and glared at the laughing secretaries. She told Joyce to notify Anthony's mother immediately.

Anthony was soon sitting quietly on a little cot. The nurse tried putting a soft ice pack around his mouth to see if this would cause his lips to contract enough to slide out of the can. But Anthony's nose was in the way and the ice packs didn't fit. Anthony never said a word, but then how could he?

Joyce suggested cutting the can off, but no one was not about to go near a child's face with a sharp object. The realization that they would have to go to the emergency room slowly sunk in.

After none of the remedies worked the principal announced "I'm calling the police!" He turned on his heel, and resolutely marched into his office banging the door shut.

Who was going to be arrested? The teacher for chatting? Anthony for sucking? The truck driver for sinking? Almost immediately a wailing police siren started softly then got closer and closer. Everyone could hear the bleep, bleep, bleep, as the car went through the red light at the intersection by the superintendent's office.

The police turned off the siren when they pulled into the driveway of the school and the car silently drove up in front of the building. The police dispatcher had obviously reported something urgent on the police radio, and it was monitored all over town including by the local newspaper. Had it been, "Boy stuck in can at school" or, "Tot trapped at Hilltop?"

Two officers strode into the office. Both were tall and had perfect posture. Neither had a wrinkle in their dark blue uniforms. The officers appeared totally unaffected by the sizzling heat as if the law were immune to the temperature.

"Anthony is in here," the nurse said, pointing to the tiny child who was wringing his t-shirt between his thumbs.

"Okay, Anthony," a giant cop said, kneeling down in front of our boy. "Let's see if we can't get you out of there." He reached into his pocket and pulled out a church key can opener. Holding the soda can securely in one hand he used the sharp point of the opener to puncture the can's bottom. There was an instantaneous rush of air, a psst, and Anthony's little lips popped out. Other than a circle of bright pink in the shape of a keyhole around his lips he was unharmed and smiling.

By the time his mother arrived, Anthony was calmly drinking a glass of ice water from a paper cup. When she finally understood what had happened, the corners of her mouth turned up for the first time all year.

"He is always into something or other," she said dryly, rolling her eyes.

"Well, I've never seen anything like this," the principal said. "He's a great kid though, very creative."

"He's a handful at home," she sighed.

"He's a handful here, too," he said. "But, he'll be fine, you'll see."

The director added, "He is bright and he is sweet. We'll work together to find some good ways to manage him."

"Thank you," Anthony's mother said pointedly to the building principal as she led her son out of the building.

Anthony was quite a celebrity on the playground during the last few days of school that year. Kids would point to him and say "That's the kid that sucked his lips into a can. The police had to come and get it off."

"Wow."

He seemed calmer in class and actually assumed an air of quiet control. He basked in all the attention and made several new friends with kids who wouldn't have anything to do with him before. The principal brought a can opener to school and put it in his top desk drawer.

Graduation ceremonies were held in the front courtyard of the school instead of on the soccer field. It was still so hot that night people were grateful not to have to walk very far.

ESSENTIAL UNDERSTANDINGS

- Under the Individuals with Disabilities Education Act, parents of children with disabilities have procedural rights. They can bring a lawsuit in federal court when they disagree with the evaluation or the special education program offered for their child.
- The IDEA mandates a free and appropriate public education; however, *appropriate* has never been defined. Conflicting ideas about what is an appropriate education have made special education the most litigated area in education.
- Attention Deficit Hyperactivity Disorder is not one of the fourteen categories of disability in the IDEA.

- When the IDEA was reauthorized in 2004, the category of Other Health Impaired, was revised to include a description of some of the symptoms of ADHD.
- According to the Centers for Disease Control and Prevention (CDC), 9.5 percent of children three years old to seventeen years old have been diagnosed with ADHD. It is relatively unknown in Europe and other countries.
- Many special education teachers believe that telling a child that they have an impairment is detrimental to their self-esteem and expectations diminish. Others feel that medication and classification allow the child to reach their full potential. The debate continues.

FOUR

The Secrets of Silence

Since we have two ears and one mouth we should listen twice as much as we talk. —Tom Leher

Recently, as many as fifty thousand migrant children from Central America have entered the United States without their parents. A 2014 *Washington Times* article titled "Illegal Border Children Taxing Resources inside U.S. Schools" reports that more than thirty-seven thousand have been released to sponsors, but that is only the beginning of the story. Despite the paralysis in Washington, DC, about what to do when a child arrives at the door to a public school, the door must be open. The school is obligated to enroll any child who lives in the community, regardless of his or her immigration status. Immigrant students often pose myriad problems in our schools that require more than additional educational services.

Separation anxiety and academic problems are common. Many speak indigenous languages, but translators are expensive and not readily available. Some children are fearful and withdrawn, others are angry and defiant. Schools are crowded: there is not enough space, not enough teachers, not enough books or desks and so, rather than welcoming immigrants who are anxious to attend school, many districts do not greet these students eagerly.

Teachers feel badly about this, they love children and believe that a good education is the key to a better life, but resources are already stretched with the children who are already here. Often teachers and administrators do not feel they know how to work with children from nonnative families, and this may be based on misguided assumptions.

This is the story of Ming Eng who came to the United States from China as a young girl with her brother, Chang. The director of special services in the district was responsible for the hundreds of children with

handicaps, the school nurses, the speech, occupational, and physical therapists, as well as the child study team who evaluated and supported
children with special needs. She was also responsible for the English as a
Second Language (ESL) program. The director supervised two ESL teachers and the sixty immigrant students who were learning English.

In this working-class community, the superintendent and others were
not pleased about the immigrant families who moved into town. He was
not eager to spend local dollars for families who many suspected were
illegal and not paying taxes. Board of education members were concerned that if extensive services were provided to immigrants, the community would be flooded with other such families.

Asking for additions to the miniscule ESL budget was always met
with serious displeasure. The local residents did not welcome families
from other countries, especially poor ones. There was an unspoken and
highly negative perception of immigrant families. Ming Eng and her
brother challenged these notions.

A day after Halloween, Ming and Chang arrived at the Gordon School
with their parents to register. Both mother and father were diminutive
and wore clothes that were much too big for them. Mr. Eng's thin arms
were buried in the numerous folds of the printed shirt he wore. Mrs. Eng
looked startled like a bird that had flown into a room through an open
window—furtive, trying to make sense of her surroundings. Neither
spoke a word of English.

Their landlord, the owner of the Chang Palace restaurant on 11th
Avenue, met with the building principal, Mr. Banton, and Jeanne, the
director of special services and English as a second language classes. The
landlord said he had rented the Eng family an apartment in a house on
East Street and presented the signed lease with a slight bow. He appeared
to know that public schools must accept children, without regard to their
immigration status, as long as they have proof that they live in the school
district.

The landlord then explained that Ming and Chang were twins and
that their parents would be working in his restaurant. He did not know
the dialect they spoke and could not help with any information other
than that they had arrived from the Fuzhou region in China a few days
earlier. "They do not speak Cantonese or Mandarin," he said. "Fujianese
is another dialect, and I don't understand it."

Funds were never put in the tight school budget to hire translators,
and Mr. Banton and Jeanne really never even considered hiring one.
Since even the landlord didn't know Fujianese, they would have to hire a
professional translator from an agency. These cost 150 dollars an hour
with a three-hour minimum plus transportation time. If a translator was
hired for every family who could not speak English, the cost would be
almost fifty thousand dollars a year.

This small district would need to fire a teacher in order to get money like that for the ESL program! Mr. Banton and Jeanne simply assumed these parents would not have anything of importance to say about their children, and no one argued with them. On that first day, these parents were dismissed as simple, poor people who knew nothing of importance to teachers, without another thought.

After the massacre at Tiananmen Square in 1989, President George H. W. Bush granted "enhanced consideration" to asylum applications from China, due to the country's strict regulations regarding one child per family. Most of these immigrants were brought into the United States by a *shetou*, or snakehead, who charged thousands of dollars to move migrants from China into the United States. Typically, after a desperate sea voyage in the hold of a ship, the migrants borrowed money to pay the snakehead back, thus indenturing themselves for years. In his 2003 book, *God in Chinatown: Religion and Survival in New York's Evolving Immigrant Community*," Kenneth Guest, an anthropologist at Baruch College, estimates that 300,000 immigrants from the Fuzhou region now reside in the United States with the largest concentration in the New York City area.

Betty, the school nurse, stepped out of the tiny closet-sized room that served as her clinic in the overcrowded school, and gave both children a practiced glance. She handed Mrs. Eng the form to get free immunizations against measles, mumps, pertussis, and typhus at the office of public health, down the street from the Chang Palace. Mrs. Eng looked at her husband before taking the paper into both hands and holding it carefully on her lap.

When Principal Banton asked how old the twins were, both parents nodded and bowed deeply, but neither spoke. He decided they should both be placed into first grade, his usual solution for children who did not speak English, even though Ming was much taller than Chang. He seemed more like a kindergarten child as he wandered about the office and watched the Xerox machine with fascination. Ming sat quietly with her head curling down over her swan-like neck.

Both children were placed into several sessions a week of ESL. As his father led him into the hall, Chang waved goodbye to everyone. He pointed to the children's pictures that lined the walls and touched each one, gently, reverently, as he passed by. Ming took tiny steps behind her mother, head down, the shuffling of her feet the only sound she made.

Staff members quickly saw something odd about the twins. Ming was at least a head taller than her twin brother, but she would not speak. Not one single sound emerged from her thin, pale lips. No cries, no sighs, and no laughter. In only a few days, Chang was already saying simple words with a big smile. Both children were eligible for the free lunch program, and the lunchroom aides made sure that every child had a tray full of governmentally determined rations. Ming never touched her food, but Chang ate every bite of the grilled cheese sandwiches. He poured catsup (the vegetable) all over his potato puffs from the tinfoil packages. He chatted with friends and offered to trade his apple for cookies. He had a new shirt and a Mickey Mouse watch on his wrist.

Ming sat with her long black hair falling in front of her face as she stared at her lap. The lunch aides pinched open her milk carton and put in a straw. They offered chocolate milk and orange juice but Ming would not eat. Her long legs descended from red pants that were several inches too short, bagged at the knees and sagged at the back of her slender body. She obediently followed her class to the bathroom, but never went inside the booths. She waited by the door while Jennifer and Colleen giggled and wet their hands in the sink. Some of the teachers were beginning to think that her parents treated Ming differently than her brother.

One afternoon in mid-December, the director of special services was at the Gordon School for a meeting, and Anne Angeli, Ming's first-grade teacher asked her, "Do you have a minute?"

"For you, Anne, I have time," she said. Over the years she had learned to trust a teacher's intuition when they were concerned enough about a child to approach an administrator. Most teachers are reluctant to admit they are having difficulty with a student. When they share a failure with a child, it is important to listen.

They chatted in the hall outside Anne's classroom as twenty-eight six-year-old children raced through the wide wooden doorway after lunch. An old tennis shoe, painted gold, dangled from the top of the door-frame—a prize awarded to the class who read the most books each month.

"I am concerned about Ming Eng," Anne started, biting the inside of her lip. As soon as she began to talk about Ming, she crossed one foot in front of the other and tucked her hands into opposite elbows. Her shoulders slumped forward.

Mr. Banton had already talked with the staff at special services about Ming's withdrawn behavior. "Should we do anything?" he had asked. "Ming has been here for over a month and she still does not eat at school and she won't talk to anyone but her brother." Jeanne had counseled patience and thought she was probably traumatized by her journey from China.

Anne had already approached her principal and was now repeating her concern directly to Jeanne. "Ming won't try to say a single word, not even sounds. I say hello to her in Chinese, but she won't say anything back. I have tried everything that I can think of. I ask her to whisper in my ear, I work with her in the back of the room where I can meet with her alone. She does not talk to the other children, but I have overheard her speak to Chang when they walk home after school. He knows a lot of English words and will try to say any word. He chatters away with the other kids already. Once I asked him if Ming could talk and he said, 'She talks all the time at home.' Maybe she is just being stubborn," Anne said with a shoulder shrug.

Ming might be shy about trying to speak in English, or perhaps a selective mute, someone who has the capability of speech but chooses not to talk. It is a relatively rare condition that is usually due to some sort of trauma. Selective mutism is a childhood disorder characterized by a failure to speak in at least one social place, typically school. This brief unwillingness to talk at school is usually the result of difficulties separating from their parents or adjusting to new routines.

No one knew what circumstances had prompted Ming's parents to leave their family, their language, and their country to flee to the United States, but it could not have been good. Probably they had not flown into Kennedy Airport. It was very likely they had been hidden somehow on a freighter. The cacophony of traffic in the city streets, the overwhelming aisles of strange foods in the supermarket, and walking on pavement everywhere would be traumatic for anyone coming from a small village. It was understandable that Ming was bewildered by her new surroundings and was having difficulty adjusting. It was an obvious explanation for her silence. Paying five hundred dollars for a translator to talk with her family about why she was upset seemed like a waste of money. Selective mutism seemed like a reasonable diagnosis.

It is quite frustrating for teachers to hear that their silent child is quite a chatterbox at home; however, that is usually the case. Once, two sisters would not talk at all in school. Their parents found it as baffling as the teachers. Their father brought in a videotape of the girls singing and making fun of each other.

"The worst thing that you could do is to try and force Ming to speak," Jeanne told Anne. "She has just come from a small village in China. You can only imagine how strange she finds everything that is going on here." As if to prove the point, a pack of fifth-grade boys raced down the stairs and leaped up like gazelles to try and touch the exit sign on the ceiling.

"Don't let Mr. Banton see you," Anne called after them. They slowed down with only an occasional shove at one another. "Ming never eats or goes to the bathroom here either," her teacher continued. "Chang says she eats when they get home, but if she doesn't like our lunches, why don't her parents pack some Chinese food for her?" Anne shook her head and asked, "Does she look thin to you?"

"No more than she was when she came."

"Do you think she should have some testing to see what is wrong?"

Jeanne told Anne that she didn't think testing would give any useful information. The tests were in English, and they didn't have any tests in Chinese. Even if they could locate a test, they would be in Mandarin or Cantonese. Ming did not speak either of those dialects. It was possible that she had not even attended school in China. She wondered what kind of a school would be in a rural Chinese village.

Most likely this was an adjustment problem. Ming had new food, a noisy school, and a new language to deal with. This might even be her first encounter with flush toilets. They didn't know how terrible her journey to the United States had been. Jeanne felt she needed time to adjust. Most cases of selective mutism, if handled with gentleness, resolve themselves in time. Ming had been seeing Susan, the ESL teacher, and Jeanne promised Anne that she would go and see how Ming was doing.

Teachers are often concerned about children in their classes who do not speak English. How could a child get anything out of sitting in a room where they understood little of what was going on? Wouldn't they be better off in a special class with a few students and a teacher who could speak both their language and English?

This sounds reasonable until you consider that more than thirty-five different languages were spoken in this small school district. Farsi, Hindi, Cantonese, French, Spanish, Tagalog, and even Somali were native languages to students attending the schools. Most school districts don't have a budget for translators, let alone a special teacher for each language.

The director of special services didn't really know what they could do for a child who was having a difficult time with the transition to a new country and spoke a dialect of Chinese that even the owner of the local restaurant did not speak.

The Spanish teacher at the high school might be prevailed upon to come and help at a meeting with Spanish-speaking parents, but the district mainly relied on the students, who often picked up English quickly, or a neighbor to translate. Hiring a professional translator was very expensive.

The taxpayers in town did not appreciate people who didn't speak English, especially those who came to live in their community. Getting the funds for two district ESL teachers had been a problem, and it was always possible they would be cut from a tight budget. No one even suggested talking with Ming's parents. What would a poor Chinese immigrant know about selective mutism or child development? How could they advise professionally trained teachers about what to do? At this point, it was believed that the best approach was to keep Ming in a compassionate, stable environment, make few demands, and give her a session each day with the ESL teacher.

After their conversation, Jeanne followed Anne into the classroom and watched as she clapped once, clapped twice, and clapped three times. By the third clap, the rambunctious six-year-olds were all clapping with her—even Ming. She was in her seat in the far left corner, near the teacher's desk, and was sitting with her head bowed. She placed her hands equally on each knee after each clap. Ming gave the impression of a wooden puppet left in a sitting position while the puppeteer works another puppet. She watched alertly, however, when Anne asked if the children wanted to listen to a story.

Anne read from *Mr. Popper's Penguins,* a book about penguins who end up living in a house. Ming solemnly pointed to Mr. Popper when Anne asked her to find him in a picture. Perhaps she related to the penguins who found themselves, like her, in a strange, new environment.

Kathy Loretto's first grade, where Chang was a student, was directly across the hall. Mrs. Loretto was passing out whiteboards for a math lesson. Chang was in deep conversation at the back of the room with two other boys. He quickly responded when his teacher asked everyone to return to their seat. He skipped the long way around and back to his place near the teacher. When Kathy glanced at Jeanne standing near the door, she mouthed, "How is Chang doing?" His teacher put one thumb and two eyebrows up and nodded three times, obviously pleased with her success with her new student.

Despite a hectic schedule of meetings and an endless stream of children who needed assistance, Ming worried Jeanne. Later that week, an hour between meetings and an open parking space right in front of the Gordon School offered an opportunity for a visit.

Rain dripped down the building and outlined the old stone sign over the door that said *Girls,* marking the side entrance to one of the oldest school buildings in the state. On her way down the basement stairs, Jeanne ran into the omnipresent school principal and explained that she was going to observe Ming in her ESL class.

"She still isn't talking or eating at school," he said.

"She's probably been through a lot."

"But it's strange that Chang adapted so quickly."

"Hopefully Susan will have some thoughts—she sees them both a couple of times a week," Jeanne replied.

"Let me know," he said and continued his daily visits to the classrooms.

Luckily Susan was just finishing her last morning group when Jeanne came into the lunchroom. This was the only available place in a school built for 250 children and housing 400 where she could teach, and it was totally inappropriate. The cooks were busy in the kitchen preparing lunch, and they joked and banged pots and trays as they set up the cafeteria line that would feed the children and staff. ESL classes had to end by 11:15 a.m. when the first group of kindergarten children came in for lunch.

The background noise was very distracting, but Susan and the three Polish students across from her didn't seem to be bothered. They were playing a matching game. Each player had to make up a question about the picture on the card before they were allowed to turn over another card and make a match. "Do you like apples?" one child asked. Susan prompted another student to answer.

"Yes, I like apples."

After the children were awarded a sticker, they rushed out the door to see who could get back to their classroom first. Susan had a few minutes to talk as she headed up the stairs to get her coat and go over to the middle school. She had given up her lunch period in order to see more students. When she smiled, the little wrinkles around her mouth disappeared. New wrinkles emerged around her eyes.

"I think we should get Ming's parents in to meet with us," Susan said. Obviously she was also concerned about the little Chinese twins. "I have called that restaurant several times and whoever answers says they will talk to the parents and get back to me, but they don't. Someone there must be able to talk with them."

Susan didn't even ask about hiring a translator. They had been through this many times with other students, and she knew there was no money for it. Jeanne considered going to the superintendent, but knew he would once again say that the members of the board of education didn't appreciate all these extra expenses for immigrant children.

"I just don't understand it," Susan continued rushing her sentences to get them all in. "Why are these twins so different? Sometimes Chinese families don't want girls—I am beginning to think her parents don't care about Ming. Chang's clothes are new, hers are old. She wears those red pants every day. He has a round face—she seems so thin I wonder what she eats. If she doesn't like the food here, why don't her parents pack a lunch for her? They work in a Chinese restaurant. They have takeout!"

"Do you think she is shy?" Jeanne inquired, also concerned about why these twins were so different.

"I don't know," Susan shook her head. "I don't know if she is shy, or traumatized. Sometimes I even think she is a little stubborn. I know she talks to Chang, but she would not speak even when they were in the same ESL class. He learns so fast, I already moved him up to the intermediate group. I can't figure her out. Why don't you come during her lesson and see what you think. She won't say anything—no sounds at all—she just looks at me."

Because Ming was making so little progress, Susan had started seeing her alone twice a week in addition to the three times she saw her with a group of other first-grade students. A specific date was made for Jeanne to observe Susan while she worked with Ming.

On her way out of the building, Jeanne passed Ming's classroom and stopped by to watch. The children were putting things away in preparation for lunch and recess. Ming seemed oblivious to the noisy bustle around her. She was seated at her desk, head bent low over a large piece of white paper. She was intently drawing a yellow bee with black stripes on the tail, two double oval wings, four hairy legs and long eyelashes. Her bee had a great deal of accurate detail for a six-year-old.

When Jeanne went to watch Ming's ESL lesson, Ming was not sitting across from Susan but right next to her—in fact she was leaning on Susan's arm and her leg was flush against her teacher's. Susan had a book of pictures and was describing each scene to Ming. "This is a house. A house has a front door and windows. Now Ming, can you say house?" Ming did not speak, but her eyes moved from the book to her teacher's face. Chin tilted down, hair falling beside her mouth, Ming said nothing, but had adoration in her eyes.

"Well, you are not talking today, but someday you will, Ming!" Susan took Ming's chin gently in her hand and gave it a little wiggle. Then, there it was—a tiny smile. Susan didn't miss that wisp of a smile, and she wiggled Ming's chin a little more. "Aha," she said, "you like that huh?"

Ming's smile grew and she covered her mouth with both hands, but her eyes were shining. "I saw that, my dear, I saw you smiling," Susan laughed. "Look, now I am smiling too." The pair returned to the book, and Susan asked Ming to point to the roof, the door, and the windows. She asked Ming to show her how many windows were on the house. Ming correctly held up six fingers.

When Jeanne sat down at the table, Susan asked Ming to say hello, and her response was to nod slightly. Susan prompted and Ming pointed to tables, chairs, beds, and a television. Ming held up fingers to show how many. The lesson ended with a matching game, and Ming displayed an amazing memory and found matches to ten cards. However, she would not make up a sentence about the object pictured.

"Ming, you worked hard today so you may choose a sticker," Susan said, and another wisp of a smile crossed the face of this serious little girl. Her teacher put the carefully selected sticker of a dog on Ming's green sweater. "Go and show Miss Angeli your sticker," she said. Ming nodded and slowly walked out of the cafeteria.

"I just don't know what to do!" Susan lamented. "I have not been able to get a single sound out of Ming."

"Looks like you are doing a wonderful job," Jeanne told her. Susan frowned. And Jeanne countered her look by saying, "Ming was glued to your side and you got her to smile today. It looks as though her receptive language skills are developing nicely."

Susan packed up the game and book. "I can't understand why she is not talking at all. She is obviously intelligent and her twin brother is thriving in the intermediate English group. It doesn't make sense."

"They are just fraternal twins."

"No," she said. "Anne and I are starting to think that it is something more going on. Why is Chang dressed in new clothes but she wears the same pair of red pants day after day? Why don't they just pack her a lunch if she does not like our food? I know that many Chinese families want boys and girls are not very valuable in that culture. I wonder if they are neglecting Ming in some way."

Jeanne asked, "Does she seem abused? Any bruises?" Perhaps Susan was right, and Chang was favored as a boy—but what could be done about that? Public school teachers don't have a right to question a cultural preference for boys.

"No, she is just so thin and so quiet it seems as though she is trying to hide," Susan replied.

"She is clearly attached to you, Susan," Jeanne replied. "I'm impressed with your ability to develop a relationship with her, I know it's frustrating but you have made progress, she trusts you."

"Yes, she does seem to enjoy the lessons. She wants to sit right next to me."

"She would be in your lap if she could."

They talked about other cases of selective mutism and decided the best course of action was not to demand that Ming speak. Children learn to speak out of love, and this tiny girl was in love with her teacher. Hopefully she would start to talk with her ESL teacher, and it will spread to other people.

Every Monday afternoon Jeanne met with the district's psychologists, social worker, and learning specialists to talk about students who might need special education services. The team often felt buried by the avalanche of children with problems. Mothers who were dying of cancer, fathers who left, learning disabilities, and high school students on drugs were discussed.

Ming came up several times. These twins were such a curious puzzle. Why was Chang fitting into his new school so easily? In his few months in the United States, he managed to chatter with friends in the class. He was cheerful, confident, and a quick study; however, Ming remained withdrawn.

The psychologist suggested an evaluation to see if she would qualify for special education programs; however, there were major problems with this approach. They would have to explain to her parents that they suspected she was handicapped before she could be tested. If they preferred Chang, they could see Ming as even more worthless if told she had a disability.

The Individuals with Disabilities Education Act (IDEA) first passed in 1974 is a special education entitlement law. Once comprehensive testing reveals that a child meets the criteria for eligibility, they are entitled to receive whatever programs and services they need in order to benefit from a public education. There can be no cost to the parents, and all of the child's special educational needs must be addressed. Eligibility is a key component of this law, and there are strict categories of eligibility, including intellectual impairment, blindness, hearing impairment, learning disabilities, or developmental disabilities.

Each of these categories has a very specific list of qualities that must be met. Ming was neither blind nor deaf. She appeared to have normal intelligence. Children who have difficulty learning that cannot be explained by other reasons, can be classified as learning disabled—however, there are very specific restrictions in this category. When making an eligibility decision, the IDEA does not allow a student to be determined to have a disability if the determining factor is a lack of instruction in reading, math, or limited English proficiency. Children cannot be classified as learning disabled just because they don't speak English or the difficulties they have in school may be due to inappropriate or absent prior education.

Since this family came from a remote area in China, it was assumed that they had not attended an educational program equivalent to those in the United States. Ming's parents had most likely paid a snakehead great sums of money in order to escape their home in China. They obviously came to seek a better life for themselves and their children. If the schools and opportunities for children in Fujian were any good, they would not have risked so much.

Even if a learning disability was suspected, a standardized test was necessary to prove it, and there were no tests in Fujianse. The standardized test most schools use to determine a learning disability, the Woodcock Johnson, was normed in the United States. This test had been translated into Spanish and, when needed, the district would hire someone to administer it. This cost about one thousand dollars. Cantonese and Mandarin Chinese are as different as English and French; however, they both use the same pictographs. If Fujianse was even a written language, the Woodcock Johnson had not been translated into this obscure dialect.

Ming's silence might have been based on trauma, but in order to classify her as emotionally disturbed she had to display an inability to learn that cannot be explained by intellectual, sensory, or health factors; an inability to build or maintain satisfactory interpersonal relationships with peers and teachers; or inappropriate types of behaviors or feelings under normal circumstances. Ming, however, caught on quickly to classroom events, had developed a relationship with her ESL teacher, and the trauma of her travel to the United States with a smuggler could certainly explain some of her fears.

The IDEA makes no provision for early intervention to help children before their problems become serious. Under the law, you either are, or you are not, handicapped. There is no middle ground for children who, if they do not receive short-term assistance, stand a chance of becoming worse. Like the medical model that does not pay for preventive care, the IDEA only allows school districts to provide services to children who are determined to be handicapped under one of the fourteen classifications. More troubling, her parents would have to agree that she is disabled. There was clearly something wrong; however, would the problem be made worse by identifying her as a handicapped child?

Noble laureate Amartya Sen wrote that 100 million women in China and India are missing, based on the unusual number of males in those countries. This is most likely due to female infanticide. Occasionally families will simply kill female infants due to a strong cultural preference for males. Many parents, especially those from different cultural backgrounds, were alarmed at the suggestion that their child was handicapped. If Ming's parents were told that she was handicapped, they might focus all of the limited family resources on Chang and any neglect of her could get worse.

Despite hopes that things would be better after the spring break in March, Ming returned to her first-grade class silent and withdrawn. Mr. Banton and Anne were very concerned, and one afternoon after school they drove to the address the parents had given as their residence. No one answered the door, and there were several dirty mattresses scattered on the floor inside.

They went to the Palace restaurant hoping someone there could translate for them. Both parents were working in the kitchen chopping vegetables. Chang was sitting at the table with a small knife helping. He bowed to Mr. Banton, his eyes wide. "Hello, Mr. Banton," he said smiling. "I am helping in the kitchen."

Mr. Eng banged on a door that opened to a steep wooden staircase down to a basement storage room and went back to work. Ming came up the stairs but stood in the doorway staring shyly. The cook explained that Ming and Chang came over to the restaurant after school and stayed until the parents finished in the kitchen after the restaurant closed. They had a small room in the basement to play.

Anne was outraged, and she called Jeanne to report on their attempt to speak with Ming's parents. "Is that any way to treat children? No wonder Ming can't talk."

"Anne," Jeanne reminded her, "Ming can talk—she chooses not to. These parents cannot be judged based on our own ideas about raising children. They have to work—they probably owe a lot of money to the *shetou* who brought them here. What are they supposed to do with their kids? They can't stay home alone."

"I think we should put Ming in a special education class," Anne opined. "She is still not speaking and something is wrong with that child."

This was not an easy solution since Ming did not fit into any of the disability categories. Telling her parents that she is handicapped and unable to do well was problematic. Generally, children who do not speak English at home or who have not been in school previously are given a year to determine the rate of learning. How fast do they learn to speak English? Jeanne promised Anne that in September, if little or no progress has been made, they could make a better determination about a possible handicap.

She promised to place Ming on the special services watch list. They would check back each month to see how she was doing. "She is better off in a general education classroom where everyone speaks and learns normally than she would be in a special class with children who are severely disabled," Jeanne told her first-grade teacher.

"She would get more individual attention in the small class at the other school," Anne replied, never one to give up on a student.

"That is true, but she has a strong relationship with Chang and she might be further traumatized over the loss of her brother if she went over to the self-contained classroom at Allen School. It would be another transition for her—when we don't really know what the problem is."

As the summer vacation approached, Anne became more and more upset about a little girl who still sat without eating in the lunchroom and who stood outside the stalls of the bathroom. She never took a drink from the fountain. Chang was reading and taking books out of the library. He had several friends and laughed and sang in his first-grade class. Anne wondered about families who could treat a boy and a girl so differently and what would happen when school was out for the summer. Chang came to school with a new t-shirt and shorts, but Ming still wore her baggy red pants.

Anne felt it was her duty to report suspected child neglect to the Division of Youth and Family Services (DYFS). One afternoon after school she called the agency without telling anyone at the school. She decided that something had to be done and that it was her responsibility to take some action for this poor little girl. She called the abuse hotline that was given to all teachers and reported what she had witnessed.

The next morning, another rainy day in May, Jeanne began her day at the high school; however, the office secretary signaled as she walked in the door. "They need you over at Gordon School," she said. Jeanne came behind the counter and dialed Connie, the special services secretary. "What's up?" she asked.

"Trouble," Connie told her and quickly continued as if there was a fire. "We got trouble right here in River City. Teacher called the abuse hotline on Ming Eng's parents. The police went to the restaurant and brought them to school. They think they have been arrested and are sitting there waiting for an interpreter."

"Well, tell them I'll be right over," Jeanne blurted, angry and confused about why Ming's teacher had called the authorities. Teachers are required to report suspected abuse, but typically they discussed their concerns with the principal or the school nurse first. They had a right to make a call even if no one agreed with them, but reporting Ming's parents for child neglect had never been considered. Jeanne was angry because she didn't see how a formal accusation of child neglect was going to help in this situation and feared it would only make things worse for Ming.

She hoped she would be able to find a parking spot near the school and also hoped she would have to drive around for a while. It would give her some time to think.

The social workers at the Division of Youth and Family Services are as overwhelmed with problems as the public schools. They don't have many options unless a child is physically being beaten. What they would be able to do in this situation was a puzzle. However Anne had some good reasons for contacting them. The law obligated teachers to report suspected neglect—it just didn't obligate enough resources to do much about it.

Jeanne didn't have to ring the security bell and wait for someone to buzz her into the building; they were watching for her. "It's bad; they are all in the library," Susan said when she met Jeanne at the door.

"Fill me in," she said, as they walked down to the school library. This was ominous. There were no rooms at the Gordon School for meetings, every available space was used for instruction. Meetings had to be held after school in classrooms, there was simply no empty space to hold meetings during the school day. If there were only a few people, meetings could be held in the principal's office and Mr. Banton would patrol the halls; however, more than four people required closing the library and the children would not get to use it. This was a very real disappointment for children eager to choose a new book to take home.

Usually when someone called DYFS to report child neglect, a caseworker would come to the school and talk to the child and the teacher. If they wanted to look for any bruises, the school nurse would be present. The caseworker would then proceed to the home to speak to the parent. Typically school personnel never heard the result of the investigation. Occasionally the child would not appear in school again; however, usually the child would simply come to class the next day. It was unusual for DYFS to hold a meeting.

Susan explained that Anne was convinced that Ming was neglected because she was female while her brother was encouraged and promoted as a male. Chang had arrived back to school on Monday sporting a new baseball cap while Ming had started to smell like Chinese food. It broke her teacher's heart to see Chang bounce down the hallway with all of his friends and gobble down pizza and peaches while Ming shuffled silently behind her classmates and sat with her hands folded in her lap and her head on her chest. When children brought in birthday cupcakes for the class, Ming would wrap hers up and bring it home. Anne had reported her concerns to DYFS.

"Anne told me that she didn't care if Chinese culture says that girls are worthless," Susan reported. "This family lives in the United States now, and they have to adopt our culture. We don't treat girls like that."

Jeanne didn't think this was going to help. Worried that Ming's parents might be angry at her for getting them in trouble with the authorities, she didn't think DYFS was going to be able to help in a situation like this.

Susan continued, "Anne called DYFS yesterday, and a social worker was already here this morning when school opened. She looked at both Ming and Chang and decided to talk to their parents. Mr. Banton explained that there is no way to get in touch with them and they don't speak a language that anyone understands. The DYFS caseworker called the police and they brought the parents here."

Mr. Banton had quickly contacted a translation service, and they agreed to find someone who could understand Fujianese. Since DYFS was involved, the superintendent was not going to argue about the cost of the translator. In a way, everyone was glad that something was happening—however trying to gain the trust of parents after the school had accused them of child abuse would not be easy.

A school library is usually a happy place. Children listen to a story and little hands pull large picture books off the shelves. They watch while the back page of the book is carefully stamped with a due date. One line of children marches out hugging carefully selected books, another eagerly waits at the door ready for a trip to enchantment. The library is one of the few places expressly designed to give children a choice.

This morning there were no smiling children fidgeting in the hall. The sound of suppressed sobbing made Jeanne want to call Connie and see if there wasn't some other emergency that demanded immediate attention. Two of the large oak tables had been pushed together in the middle of the room. Mrs. Eng sat next to her husband and was weeping. Mr. Eng waited with his eyes down and his hands on his knees. Exactly the way that Ming sat.

The DYFS social worker was in her forties with brown hair tucked in back of her ears. She sat looking straight ahead with her arms crossed in front of her chest. Although she was leaning back into the chair, she projected alertness.

Two police officers stood to the side of the low bookcases, and one of them was Tommy, Connie's son. He had just knocked a monkey puppet, Curious George, off the top of the bookcase, and was trying to rearrange the puppet and the book back to their original position.

Anne and Mr. Banton sat on the other end of the table. He had his chin in his hand and was leaning on the table. He seemed to have as much time as it would take to get some perspective on this issue. Anne looked grim. So much for being anonymous. Every single time a teacher called DYFS to report suspected abuse, the families quickly found out who had called.

"We are waiting for the translator," Susan whispered as if to explain the portentous silence broken only by Mrs. Eng's muffled sobs.

"Good God," Jeanne said into Susan's ear. "Where is the translator coming from?"

"Cherry Hill, I think," she sighed. That was clear on the other side of the state. This would be a miserable morning, and travel time and translation services would be very expensive.

Mr. Banton's secretary, Elaine, appeared at the door. She caught his eye and asked if he knew where Jimmy Otis's saxophone was. "The music teacher is here," she said.

"It's under my desk—his mother thought his lesson was yesterday and she left it with me," he replied. Abuse cases, saxophone cases, and cases of milk—the principal knows about every single thing that happens in the building.

The woman from DYFS sat patiently and looked as though she wasn't moving until she got some information.

The relief was palpable when almost an hour later a Chinese man finally swept through the door in a long trench coat. You could smell cigarette smoke on it, and he put it over the back of a chair because there was no coatrack. Mr. Zhang bowed stiffly from the waist as he was introduced to everyone, and he took a seat next to Mr. and Mrs. Eng. Everyone shifted a little in their seats. Mrs. Eng cried a little louder. Perhaps his appearance made her even more frightened.

The DYFS caseworker explained the reason for the meeting. Mr. Zhang listened carefully and looked slowly at each person in the room, his face a blank slate. He turned and began to speak softly to the Engs. Mrs. Eng stopped crying, and they talked for a while.

"I have explained to Ming's parents that you feel she is being neglected," he said. "Her mother wants you to know that she loves her daughter very much. She would never ever harm her in any way," he announced to a very attentive audience. "I have explained that they are not arrested." Mr. Eng sat up in his chair for the first time. What a difference to be able to speak—to explain. Without language we are trapped inside our fears.

Mr. Zhang continued with an amazing story. "Ming's mother wants you to know that she risked her life to save her daughter in China." No one had expected to hear anything like this. The DYFS social worker folded her hands in her lap. Suddenly several assumptions had been tossed right off the table.

"In China you are allowed to have only one child, unless you have twins. When Ming was born, her mother knew that her mother-in-law would be very upset if she brought home a girl and might even try to kill her baby. She decided to hide her daughter to protect her. She left the hospital and came home when her mother-in-law was not there. She put her baby girl in a closet and wrapped her tightly so she could not move or cry. She told everyone that the baby died in the hospital."

Anne and Susan both looked up at the ceiling and blinked back tears as they tried to absorb this very different information. Mr. Zhang continued to an incredulous audience. "Whenever she could, she fed Ming and cared for her, but she kept her tightly wrapped so she would not harm herself or make any sounds."

Everyone in the room was mesmerized by this story. No one had even considered anything like this. Ming's shyness in the noisy school, especially the cafeteria and bathrooms now made sense. Her inclination to eat only once a day, her reluctance in the bathroom. Her parents had just been blamed for her behavior; no other explanation had ever been considered. Everyone in the room had to confront assumptions about people from a place they did not know.

Mr. Zhang let this information sink in and then continued. "Mrs. Eng had a plan and she quickly got pregnant again. She hoped this next child would be a boy and it was. She presented her mother-in-law and the local authorities with Ming and Chang and said that they were twins!"

Anne was biting her lips and pushing into the corners of her eyes to stem the tears.

The interpreter raised a slender hand above the oak table and gestured around the room. "When the authorities suspected this was not true, she sent Ming away to live with a relative, but she missed her daughter too much. She wants to know why you think she would hurt this daughter who she loves more than her own life."

This question hung in the air waiting for an answer. There was no good answer. Why don't we examine our negative opinions about people who are not like us? Finally Jeanne tried to explain, "We did not understand why Ming was so different from Chang. We wondered why she didn't eat anything or wear new clothes like he does."

When the translator posed this question to Mrs. Eng, she became animated for the first time tapping her chest and raising her shoulders. Mr. Zhang translated, "Her mother says that Ming does not like American food and she is too shy to use chopsticks at school, so she will not bring Chinese food from home. She refuses to wear her new clothes to school because she is afraid they will get dirty. Her mother says she is very stubborn and will not listen. She is sorry."

With this revelation Ming's behavior made more sense. It was like being lost and finally seeing something familiar and how to get back. "We want Ming to do well, and we didn't know how to help her," Jeanne said. "Now we understand better why she is so quiet. I hope you will forgive us," she nodded at Ming's parents.

During the translation Mrs. Eng relaxed her shoulders and looked at the people gathered about the table for the first time. Her shy glance forgave those who get frustrated with children who don't respond to good intentions and lapse into blaming the parents. Everyone had just assumed Ming was neglected since she was so withdrawn. Why don't we assume that parents from other cultures mirror our own devotion to our children?

The translator gave Mr. Banton his business card. There would be a big bill for his travel and services; however, there was now a way to communicate with the family. "Let me know and I can call and tell them what you need," Mr. Zhang said. "I would like to help this family," he repeated as he put on his coat.

The police took the Engs back to the restaurant, and the teachers met to decide how to help Ming. When you realize a mistake, there is nothing better than being able to do something to rectify it. Instead of testing, determining what the problems are, and then deciding what kind of special help children need, perhaps another question was required. "Where do you think that Ming would feel the most comfortable?" Jeanne asked.

Various classes were discussed. She could stay in the first grade and have speech therapy, physical therapy, and occupational therapy and time in the resource center for small-group academic instruction. That would pull a shy, hesitant child in several different directions each day.

She could be moved to the Allen School in a special class for young children with neurological problems. These children were learning colors and how to count. They played with puppets and in the toy kitchen. Although the activities were good for learning English, Ming would have to go to a new school and would not be with her brother. Her parents might not agree to this.

A third option was to put Ming with older children in a small self-contained special education classroom at the Gordon School. Due to her early experiences there was a good possibility she was older than six. Alexi Kwo, the special education teacher, was soft-spoken, kind, and married to a Chinese man. Best of all, she ran a very quiet classroom. She had even asked if Ming could be in her class.

Placing children into classes where the teacher will take a special interest in them is not part of the special education law, but Washington, DC, is a long way away. When you don't know what else to do, following your heart is a good direction to take. The team decided to keep Ming in her first-grade class for the last month of school, but have her visit Mrs. Kwo's special education class every day and increase the time she spent there. It wasn't legal according to the IDEA, but it was exactly what a traumatized child like Ming needed. They would worry about the law later.

Ming entered Mrs. Kwo's class full-time in September with a new Minnie Mouse lunch box and a thermos of egg drop soup. She had a yellow bow in her hair. With careful instruction from Mrs. Kwo, Ming learned to point to the letters in the alphabet, then to sight words. She drew and wrote easily and soon could do single digit addition and subtraction. She began to speak softly to her ESL teacher, then she said her letters to Mrs. Kwo.

Everyone celebrated her progress. One day, Mrs. Kwo actually heard her sing the daily good morning song along with the class. Ming had been mouthing the words for a few weeks, but on this day Ming had forgotten her fear and her words, connected by the melody, were audible.

On Halloween Jeanne liked to visit the schools to see the costumes and feel the excitement. She saw so many children with problems in her job; she felt it was important to also experience the fun of childhood. She had heard that Ming was talking a little and was eager to see her. However, on that exciting day, Ming was cowering in a corner. Her classmates were in full costume regalia and bounding around the room as goblins, Spider-Man, and Dora the Explorer.

"Ming is terrified," her teacher explained. "She does not understand about Halloween and what all the excitement is about. We are all supposed to be in the parade, but she refused to wear a costume and I can't just leave her alone in the classroom."

While Mrs. Kwo took the frenzied children down to line up in the costume parade, Jeanne stayed with Ming who began to sob when everyone left the room. She eventually went to the window where they watched everyone lining up to march in the Halloween parade around the school yard. She seemed upset by all the noise and excitement, but she also wanted to be part of it.

"Do you want to be in the parade, Ming?" Jeanne asked. She nodded wistfully, yes, but Ming did not have a costume. How she could participate without being in the midst of the pushing and laughing children? Jeanne looked around the room for some inspiration and her eyes caught the American flag hanging over the blackboard. Climbing on the teacher's desk, much to Ming's delight, she yanked the flag out of its holder and handed it to Ming. "Here you go. You can lead the parade with the American flag! Would you like to do that?" Walking in front of the parade would keep her out of the excited crowd.

"Yes," she said, and Ming's dark eyes were shining. She held the flag with her two arms out in front of her waving it back and forth, watching it flap.

"It's a great costume for you, Ming," Jeanne said. "You will be an immigrant."

Ming adjusted well in the self-contained special education class. She was never very talkative; however, she loved her teacher and she loved to draw. She progressed from first grade to fifth grade, making good progress.

A special program was planned for her in middle school. There she had small special education classes in English, math, and social studies, but after a few weeks she retreated into silence and stopped eating. She needed a small self-contained class and since the district did not have one, she attended a special private school for young girls with emotional problems. The community never balked at any expense to help a child with a handicap.

After a few years she returned to the high school and earned her diploma. She planned to go to community college, and wanted to be a teacher. Her brother was the valedictorian of his high school class and studied to become a doctor. Her parents eventually owned the Chang restaurant. They bought a house in town and installed a three-tiered fountain in the front yard ornamented with dragons and foo dogs. It was the best house on the block.

ESSENTIAL UNDERSTANDINGS

- This incident demonstrates how caring teachers and school providers can be ineffective without understanding students' families.
- Parents of children with special needs can be marginalized by professionals who often do not expect or encourage them to be active providers of information. This is compounded when parents are poor and when they do not speak English.
- The knowledge barrier about special education procedures and programs is another significant obstacle.
- Research has identified many barriers minority families face, including cultural differences in understanding disabilities, cultural differences in expectations of participation, access to information, negative professional attitudes toward parents.
- The IDEA does not allow a student to be classified with a disability if the determining factor is a lack of instruction in reading, math, or limited English proficiency. Children cannot be classified as learning disabled because they don't speak English or due to inappropriate or absent prior education.
- In order to be classified as emotionally disturbed, children must display an inability to learn that cannot be explained by intellectual, sensory, or health factors; an inability to build or maintain satisfactory interpersonal relationships with peers and teachers; or inappropriate types of behaviors or feelings under normal circumstances.
- Teachers are legally required to report suspected neglect or child abuse to family service agencies. However, unlike physical abuse, reporting neglect may have unintended consequences especially when different cultures are involved.

FIVE

Drug Bust

You can observe a lot by just watching.
—Yogi Berra

Special education departments are full of passionate staff. Nurses, instructional aides, English as a second language (ESL) teachers, preschool teachers, resource center teachers, special class teachers, psychologists, learning disability teacher consultants, social workers, speech teachers, occupational therapists, and physical therapists are ardent about their student's needs and they complain when things are not right.

"My classroom computer is so old I can't use software with pictures."

"What can we do about the science department? They treat me like a criminal and won't let me borrow one lousy microscope for my science class."

"You're crazy if you think special education students should take the state tests. They will cry with frustration. They can't do a single question—what is the point of that?"

"Why do I have to cover classes when general education teachers are absent? I have to cancel my own students."

"Why do the special class kids have to have gym with each other? Can't they be integrated with the other kids for that one class?"

Danna taught a self-contained class for students with developmental disabilities at the high school. She was passionate about her students and also had many ideas about how to better integrate them into the school and the community. One afternoon after school, she peered into the supervisor of special education's office. "Do you have a minute?"

"Only for you Danna, only for you," Jeanne, the school district supervisor, responded.

Danna, dark hair, perky smile, and quirky presence, walked with her typical quick step into the office and sat in the chair at the side of Jeanne's desk. She pushed the pile of papers aside to make room for her elbow and rested her chin on it.

"What's up?"

"I've been thinking."

"Okay, now I'm in trouble. I thought we talked about this and you were not going to continue thinking of things—at least things that involve me."

"Jeanne, this is important."

"I'm listening," she said, then called out to her secretary in the outer office. "Connie, if the president calls, tell him I'll get back to him, Danna is here."

"Okay," Danna sighed, brushing the joke aside with her tone of voice. "You know, I don't get why our kids only get gym once a week and the regular kids have it every day."

Jeanne reexplained that the physical education (P.E.) teachers only had time in the schedule for one extra physical education period a week. However, next year they left more room for the students in the special education class that Danna taught. The building principal was not willing to change the entire schedule for six kids with disabilities.

"Okay," Danna started, "but why do they have to have a special class? Why can't they go to gym with the other kids? What is it about gym anyway? My kids can run around and throw balls. Are they poison?"

Jeanne thought about reminding Danna that the gym teachers seemed to feel like their subject was not valued. They were very sensitive about being asked to do anything differently than the subject-area teachers. Any comments such as "it's just gym" would almost certainly evoke offense and cause the teachers to feel belittled.

"Danna, I have done all that I can this year; I just don't think that anything can change. The schedules are all set. Maybe next year."

"I have another idea," Danna interrupted, taking her hand down and spreading her fingers across the desk. "Roseanne is good physically. She is coordinated, she can catch a ball, ride a bike, and she is a good bowler. She shoots hoops with her brothers. Why can't she participate in a regular gym class? What do they do that involves reading? Even if it did involve reading, she would get the physical training and a chance for the high school kids to see that the kids in my class are not monsters."

Danna had a point. Special education teachers had worked hard to develop specialized curriculum for children with disabilities. They did not take general education classes when they could not keep up with normally developing peers. They taught essential reading like signs, making change, and telling time so that students could function independently. They taught work skills such as cooking, sorting, and cleaning.

The regular education initiative, spearheaded by Madeline Will, associate commissioner of special education for the U.S. Department of Education, recommended that students with disabilities be included in regular education classes as much as possible. Federal laws required school districts to develop transition programs for students with special needs. The definition of education had expanded beyond reading, history, and math. Students with special needs should be prepared to live and work in the community. They were expected to contribute as much as they could. These skills were mandated in the revised Individuals with Disabilities Education Act (IDEA).

Danna had posed a good question; why did students in self-contained special education classes have to stay together all the time? Couldn't some of them take a class or two with the general population? It was a good question; however, adding a student with developmental disabilities to a regular class would be met with outright horror.

Schools often operate like a medieval fiefdom surrounded by a moat to keep changes out. Each and every new idea is met with mistrust, controversy, and suspicion. Most teachers wanted a perfect class of intelligent, motivated students; so they "could teach." They didn't want students who struggled. That, however is a mythical class. There are high- and low-performing students in every classroom. Why don't teachers see unusual students as a challenge instead of just a problem? Why does our educational system only reward success? Isn't improvement the real goal?

Jeanne had discussed this with the high school supervisors. Herb, the head of the math department, put it well. He said, "Let me know when the board of education stops wanting me to tell them who the valedictorian is. My job is sorting students."

Special education teachers were also doubtful about including students with special needs in general education classes. They wondered what a student with intellectual impairments would do in a general education classroom except sit in the back. General education teachers were even more opposed to the idea of inclusion. They asked, "What is a kid who is retarded going to learn in a class with regular kids? They need very specific instruction, not Shakespeare or the Greeks and Romans."

Danna continued. "Jeanne, have you ever seen that special gym class? The kids sit there most of the time. Some of my students could be good at sports if they had a chance. Just because a person has an intellectual disability, doesn't mean they don't have physical skills."

Danna had a point. Students were pushed and encouraged in P.E. to do their personal best athletically. Roseanne did have some athletic skills. Why not let her take a gym class with the other kids? It might cut down on the stares when students saw her in the hallway, the lunchroom, or the bathrooms. No other students ever sat at the lunch table with the kids from the self-contained class.

"What teacher could we get who would let Roseanne join their P.E. class?" Jeanne asked. The P.E. teachers had not been pleased about teaching the special education students in the first place.

"I already suggested this to Kathy," Danna said. Kathy was an energetic, cheerful teacher who also had a newborn niece with Down syndrome. She and Danna had become friends, and she often visited the special class during her free periods. Would this be a viable option?

"I think we should just try it for a few days and see if there are problems we haven't considered. If it works out; we will continue," Jeanne said. She wisely thought they would have a better chance of acceptance if this proposal was presented as simply an experiment. She could imagine the reaction of the P.E. department chairperson when approached. However, if the P.E. teacher supported it, and Roseanne had visited a couple of times, then she could say how successful it had been—not ask if it was possible. It was often better to try something new and be prepared to apologize if things went wrong than to ask for permission.

"Well, don't mention this," Jeanne remarked as Danna got up to leave. "It will be all over town—and that will be the end of it." Danna nodded and then shook her head.

Jeanne was going to ask the high school principal why every U.S. history class in the school, except her special education classes, got new books. Books for special education classes were not considered when supplies and equipment for other classes were ordered. The building principals assumed that special education funds should pay for special education needs, but the IDEA had never been fully funded.

There were only limited funds in the special education department. There was no money to pay for new history books in special education classrooms. There students used the books that had been discarded by the academic departments. Many knew they had old books and were ashamed of them.

The special education secretary interrupted, and said that Jennifer, the middle school principal, was on the phone and needed to speak to Jeanne immediately. Some principals regarded everything as urgent—even if it was only to say that they had a new ESL student enroll. The middle school principal typically didn't share much—preferring to handle things at the middle school on her own.

"Hey, Jennifer," Jeanne began, "you have already used up your allotment of referrals for special education." She used this line with all of the principals, not that it made any difference, or that it could be done. The special education department was required to consider any request for special education no matter when it came in (the last day of school) or how unlikely the student was to have special education needs (got a B in honors chemistry).

Jennifer laughed and replied, "I know, I know."

"What's up?"

"I'm not going to make your day any easier," she said and explained that she had received several phone calls from parents regarding an incident in the lunchroom the previous day. One of the classified students had made sexual comments and lewd gestures to a thirteen-year-old girl. Several lunchroom aides had also seen him throw his legs apart and do an explicit bump and grind. The girl's family members were prominent citizens with many friends in town.

The boy in question, Alex, was a recent arrival. His family was from Slovenia and had lived for a few years in a large nearby city. They had recently moved to the district. His previous school district had classified him as learning disabled and he had been in a middle school there. However, he was much taller and obviously older than a typical middle school student.

Written records from schools in Slovenia were not available, and the records from the urban district were scanty. The social worker's family history write-up explained that the family was Roma. Everything in the IDEA reports was confidential; however, Jeanne reported that many people knew the family were Roma.

When students who are classified as eligible for special education transfer from another school district, the new district must immediately follow the existing individualized education program (IEP). The diagnostic team who reviewed this case continued his placement at the middle school with some special education classes during the day.

"Parents are asking what this kid is doing here in the middle school," Jennifer reported. "He was in my office with his mother a few minutes ago and he does not deny what he did in the lunchroom. I told him not to come back to school and I am suspending him indefinitely. He doesn't belong here. He needs to be in a special school."

"You can't do that," Jeanne replied.

"Why not?"

"He is a special education student, and you can't deny him access to an education until you demonstrate that his behavior was not related to his handicap."

"Jeanne, I am letting you know what I had to do, you do what you have to do," the middle school principal said. The conversation was over.

Special education laws are quite clear that students with handicaps have due process protections. They cannot be kept out of their educational programs for more than ten days during a school year. The student could be suspended for ten days; however, he could not just be tossed out of school without a very special procedure called a manifestation determination.

King John is known as the worst king of England. He is best remembered for the Magna Carta. He was forced by his disgruntled nobles to sign it in 1215. Now over eight hundred years old, the Magna Carta has been described as the foundation of the freedom of an individual against capricious authority. It decrees that a king cannot throw people in a dungeon just because he wants to. There must be a procedure to determine guilt. This is known as due process, and it is a part of the special education law, the IDEA. The principal of the middle school, like King John, could not just throw Alex out of school. Alex was legally entitled to a determination of his guilt.

A team of special education professionals who were knowledgeable about the student needed to meet and review Alex's individualized education program. If it was appropriate and being properly implemented, then the team could determine if the student's behavior was caused by, or related to, the student's handicapping condition known as a manifestation determination. The team would decide if the educational placement needed to be changed. A building principal, the superintendent, or even the members of the school board cannot expel a student with special needs from school without due process.

The previous year, Roseanne had actually brought a can of beer to school in her lunch. She had packed her own lunch that day. She set it out on the lunchroom table and snapped open the top. A lunchroom aide had raced across the room to take it from her much to the amusement of the high school students. Although bringing alcohol to school is illegal, this incident was clearly related to her disability. She thought it was a can of soda. The determination was made by the district diagnostic team. She could not be disciplined like a regular student, but her parents did begin to store the beer in a different place.

Angry, Jeanne dialed the superintendent's number. She didn't need to remind him about the due process rights of students with special needs. But she did remind him that a special school for Alex would cost the district more than thirty thousand dollars plus the costs of transportation. She let him know that Jennifer was forcing such a placement since she would not allow the student back to school. Within a half-hour, Jennifer called back wondering what else could be done about a student who was probably a sex pervert and didn't belong in the middle school.

"Jennifer, I understand that parents don't want him in the middle school—but we have to provide an education to all students."

"Well this kid is probably sexually active, and it's not a good fit in a middle school."

"Jennifer, he's a kid—he was probably just fooling around. If you are so worried about this, I will get a psychiatric consult and let the psychiatrist tell us if he is a danger or not." Jennifer agreed reluctantly to this, but insisted that Alex remain out of school until she got the psychiatrist's report and the school diagnostic team could review it.

When she put the phone down, Jeanne asked her secretary to find the latest budget figures. She would have to come up with a way to pay for this consult, which could run over one thousand dollars. Staring at the wall did not help. Unexpected expenses like this one always used up the special education budget. There was no extra money for new history books.

On warm days the P.E. teachers kept a back door open, and later that week, Jeanne slipped into the building through the gym. She admired the games of badminton being played center court. She also found Kathy storing basketballs.

It is often useful to informally float a new idea past those who are likely to be involved. If they drop to the floor and gag, or grab you by the throat, it is not such a good idea. "What would you think of letting one of the girls in our special education class join one of your classes?" Jeanne said.

Kathy bit her bottom lip. She recalled the number of times the high school principal had ranted "these kids don't belong here" and thought of her tiny niece with Down syndrome. "Well," she said. "Danna and I have talked about this. Who are you thinking of?"

"Roseanne is quite good at sports. She plays basketball in her driveway with her older brothers. Her family takes her bowling. She runs beautifully and can catch and throw whatever ball you've got. Danna and I thought she would be able to benefit from a regular P.E. class."

"Yeah, I have seen Roseanne—she is pretty good. She listens and tries to do whatever Danna says. It's that horrid laugh—it makes her look so stupid—and she has got to keep her tongue in her mouth."

"Well, that's the point," Jeanne continued. "If we could tell her that she could be in the gym class with you, she might be more motivated to do it."

"Hey," Kathy said with a smile. "This could be cool."

Walking away, Jeanne was elated, only she didn't want Kathy to see her excitement and begin to wonder exactly what she had agreed to. She wanted to let Danna know right away. The stairs to the top floor where Roseanne's special education class was located didn't seem so hard to climb for some reason. "Hey Danna," she said. "Kathy might let Roseanne into her class!"

Danna's eyes got big. She glanced around the room and spotted Roseanne washing dishes. "Roseanne, put your tongue in your mouth and stand up straight, too."

Danna agreed that they should keep this little plan private for the time being. If the principal got wind of it, there was no doubt that it would get quashed for one reason or another. He was adamant that he had been forced to put up with the special class kids in his school. He was not happy about it, didn't feel they belonged, and wanted to make sure they did not interfere with any aspect of his high school. The superintendent might be concerned that the special student would trip and fall in a general P.E. class and the district would be liable for an injury.

Administrators have a responsibility to be seen and heard throughout school buildings. Teachers are alone for almost seven hours with a bunch of potential maniacs (the children). "Management by walking around" or

MBWA is important. Particularly in schools, it is the best way to know exactly what is going on.

Jeanne made it a practice to use the student bathrooms. Is it clean? Does everything function properly? Sometimes students wanted to hide for a moment; Jeanne wanted to know what they were hiding from. This practice yielded interesting encounters; don't students ever flush? What size child could have left that deposit? Just that week she had overheard two high school girls tell Roseanne not to shriek. She seemed to like the acoustics in the bathroom and often hung on to the sink and gave out little high-pitched shrieks.

Jeanne had been in a booth, when she overheard one of the high school girls who was carefully grooming her long brown hair say, "Roseanne, stop that. It's obnoxious."

"She can't understand you," her friend replied.

"Roseanne, do you understand me?" Roseanne must have nodded and she stopped her painful song. The brunette continued, "See—she gets it." Both girls tore rugged brown paper from the dispenser to dry their hands and hurried off to class. When Jeanne came out of the booth, Roseanne was still looking after them. Seeing Jeanne, she went back to her short shrieks. Why did she stop for the high school girls?

When Jeanne got back to her office, she noticed that a full cup of coffee was sitting on the left side of the desk. The cup read: Let Me Drop Everything and Work on Your Problem. The coffee was cold and milk scum circled the lip. Did she forget to drink it this morning or was this yesterday's coffee? She sorted through the seven phone messages on pink paper. Urgent messages were left on the chair.

She made an appointment with the district's consulting psychiatrist. The one-hour consultation and report would cost 1,200 dollars. Alex's parents would have to take their son to the psychiatrist's office. He wanted to talk to them and could do so next week. If they did not have a car or didn't drive, the district would have to figure out a way to get them to the appointment.

There was a message from Jennifer that Alex's parents had come to see her with an aunt who was quite furious that her nephew had been told to leave school.

"She is threatening to get a lawyer," Jennifer said when Jeanne called her. Even worse, Jennifer had been approached by several teachers with their union representative asking what a student like this was doing in the middle school. She had assured the teachers that the district had arranged for a psychiatrist to examine Alex. He would not be allowed to return to school if he was dangerous to himself or others due to his sexual behavior.

In the meantime Jeanne would have to get a home tutor. Alex would not be able to see the psychiatrist before he had been out of school for ten days. The special education laws are quite clear that students who are protected by the IDEA cannot be denied an education. When they are suspended from school for over ten days in any school year, the district must provide tutoring. Special needs students must receive two hours a day or ten hours a week of education. General education students, who broke a leg or could not come to school, were eligible for one hour per school day. The tutors would go to the home and cover the lessons that the student was missing in school as long as a parent or adult family member was home.

Home instruction was an effective way to keep students from falling behind. For some students, it was the first time they had close contact with a teacher. The student's own teachers were asked first if they wanted to be paid the extra hours to do the home instruction. In Alex's case, he would get to know one of his teachers, and it might help to ease his transition back into school.

Natalie was a special education teacher who had Alex in her resource center English class. She quickly agreed to tutor Alex. Her husband was out of work again, and he would be home with their children while she tutored in the afternoons after school and on Saturday. Natalie would pick up the class work and books from the middle school teachers and take them to Alex. The money for this expense would have to come out of the special education budget.

Natalie was tall, athletically built, and confident. She had earned the respect of the teachers with her dedication to her students. Students in the special education programs often learned how to manipulate their teachers who were so eager for them to do well. Natalie would have none of that. She had a direct stare that said very clearly: you can figure out this problem yourself. Alex would work hard in her presence.

After arranging for Alex's tutor, Jeanne had a message to call Kathy in the P.E. office right away. A loud voice boomed "Yo" when she called. Kathy wasn't there, and the department chair who answered wanted to know what the call was about. Jeanne was alarmed by his tone and worried that something had happened. She would have to wait until Kathy had a chance to call her back.

Teachers are not easy to reach during the school day. They are not sitting at a desk answering the phone. Teachers are responsible for student safety and are legally liable if they are negligent and something happens to a child. They need to be aware of everything that is going on in the classroom. If a teacher was on the phone and a student was injured, it would be criminal negligence.

Middle school and high school teachers have five instruction periods, one duty, and a prep period to write lesson plans. Very few ever get a chance to plan lessons during the school day. The prep period is when meetings are held, teachers try to scrounge up an extra textbook for the student who just arrived from Costa Rica, or run to the bathroom if they are lucky.

Kathy called back later that afternoon. "I don't think having one of the kids from the special class in regular P.E. is a good idea," she said. Jeanne wondered what had happened to change her mind, however, she knew better than to press her. Kathy had to live in the athletic department.

This was a very real disappointment. Danna had called Roseanne's mother to let her know about the plan to include her daughter into the general education P.E. program. She had suggested that Roseanne needed a haircut and proper gym clothes. Roseanne's mother often seemed ambivalent about her daughter. Neighbors reported that Roseanne was sometimes walking a toy baby carriage around the neighborhood late at night. Sometimes she came to school without socks or a coat in cold weather.

However, Roseanne's mother brought new gym clothes into school the very next day. Danna had been shocked, since this was not a family who was active in the school programs. She had never appeared for back-to-school night or any IEP meetings. Districts have the right to maintain a student in a special education program after parents agreed to the original placement. Roseanne had simply continued in her special education self-contained class year after year. The suggestion that she could participate in gym class with normally developing peers had motivated Roseanne's family.

Inclusion had a ripple effect. It wasn't just about motivating the student with special needs. It wasn't just about mixing with peers and helping students get to know individuals with disabilities. It wasn't just about helping general education teachers see the unique skills that special students had. It was also about helping families have different expectations for their son or daughter. It was a pretty powerful movement. However, just a simple experiment was too much to even try. Everyone was disappointed.

Later that week, Roseanne was in the hallway with Danna when they ran into Kathy and some of her students. Several of the girls from Kathy's P.E. class greeted Roseanne. One of the girls asked, "Roseanne, when you are coming to my gym class?"

Roseanne turned and asked Kathy, "When can I come to your class? Can I go tomorrow?"

Kathy sputtered for a moment, but asked her students how they knew Roseanne. It turned out that Martha lived next door and liked to shoot hoops with Roseanne and her brothers.

"I'll show you about the locker room," she told Roseanne.

Impressed with the positive reaction from her student, Kathy confided in Danna about the pressure she was getting from the rest of the department about adding Roseanne to her P.E. class. Danna convinced her that if she caved to the tenured teachers she would always be the underdog. "Stand up for what you want to do, the hell with those assholes," were Danna's savvy words of advice.

Danna and Kathy made some decisions about the experiment.

1. Roseanne would come down to the gym with the instructional aide. They would get her a locker in the locker room during lunch when few other students would be present.
2. Kathy would show her where to put her clothes and where to put her gym things. The aide would help her the first week until she could manage on her own.
3. She would join the P.E. class on the first day of the third quarter. The class would be starting a new unit on basketball. This was an area that Roseanne knew and liked.
4. The instructional aide would walk her down to the gym and pick her up after class the first few days.

Technically there should be a meeting with Roseanne's mother. She would sign a new IEP that listed the general education P.E. class. The IDEA and IEPs are not flexible. The IEP does not allow teachers to experiment with a program change to see if it might be better. An IEP is written for an entire school year, not for a week. It had to contain the goals and objectives of the educational program that would meet Roseanne's special needs and could be over twenty pages long.

A meeting to change her existing IEP would require her special education teacher, her general education teacher, her case manager, a school administrator, her parents, and Roseanne herself because she was over fourteen years old. That kind of a meeting might take weeks to schedule. Simply working with the two teachers was easy and meant the experiment could be stopped if any problems came up that had not been anticipated. Amending her IEP was too public and too complicated. It would almost certainly quash the new idea.

Roseanne asked about the gym class every single day—several times a day. Danna made a calendar, and she and Roseanne marked off each day together. Roseanne pasted a big basketball on the day when she would start going to "gym with the girls" as she called it.

On a clear Monday that promised warmer weather in the afternoon, Alex's home tutor Natalie came down to Jeanne's office. She had spent both Saturday and Sunday afternoon with Alex. "He's so trusting," she reported. "He does everything I ask, but he struggles with anything that is abstract. He is like a child in a man's body. They lived in the city before his family moved here—I think he missed a lot. He told me he was in special classes at his old school and they didn't do anything all day. He needs to get back to his classes before he gets even further behind."

"His mother took him to see the psychiatrist last week, and we should have the report soon. Once we get the report, we will have the diagnostic team review it and make a manifest determination if his behavior was related to his disability. I think he should be back in school shortly," Jeanne replied.

"That's what I wanted to talk to you about," Natalie said, leaning forward in her chair and glancing at the doorway. The door was closed.

"Are you concerned about Alex?" Jeanne asked. Had he made some sort of sexual advance toward her? Perhaps there was something unusual about this young man. Would the psychiatrist have noted it?

No matter how much training a person has, can fifty minutes of talking to a person reveal every nuance of their personality? Most kids have several different personalities depending on who they are with and the circumstances they are in. Alex's mother had taken him to see the psychiatrist. He would have been on his best behavior. Alex might have gotten more relaxed during the tutoring sessions. His tutor was young and pretty. Had he flirted with her?

"No, I'm not concerned about Alex," Natalie said adamantly. "There is something that you should know about this situation. I don't think anybody here will tell you, so I am going to."

Natalie revealed that the incident in the lunchroom had another component. The story the middle school principal had been told was edited. It seems that the girl on the other side of the lunchroom table had been teasing Alex for several weeks. She had invited him to eat lunch with her and her girlfriends. During lunch she had repeatedly run her tongue around the outside of her open mouth while closing one eye.

After asking Alex if he "wanted some," she had ducked down under the table and pressed his knees apart. She proceeded to make licking movements with her tongue and sucking noises. When she sat back down in her seat, she flicked her eyelashes at him. He responded with explicit language and the bump and grind.

"So Alex's behavior was reported, but no one said anything about what the girl did?"

"That's right," Natalie said.

"Why?" Jeanne sputtered, angry at being manipulated.

"We have this fantasy here that our little middle school kids are innocent, especially the girls. The teachers don't see what they don't expect to see. Also, this girl's family has been in town forever. Alex is an older kid who lived in the city. It got around that his family is Roma. He got identified as the problem."

"Who told you this?"

"One of my other students was at the next table and she finally told me. It's really all over the school at this point."

No wonder Alex had been blamed. He was new, foreign, and special ed.: a recipe for trouble. Social history reports were supposed to be totally confidential, but somehow this one had been leaked. The knowledge that his family was Roma was just too juicy to suppress. "Thanks, Natalie," Jeanne said as she put her hand on the telephone to call the middle school principal. How much of this story did she know?

Later that morning Jeanne realized she had forgotten entirely about Roseanne's first day in P.E. class when her secretary told her that Danna wanted her at the high school as soon as possible. Danna was waiting at the door to her classroom and she looked both upset and defeated. "Whatever happened in the gym class?" Jeanne sputtered to a black look and sunken shoulders.

"I think you better talk to Roseanne about it," Danna said.

Jeanne took Roseanne into the empty classroom next door, and they sat down facing each other. Roseanne seemed unconcerned. "What happened in gym today?" Jeanne asked.

"Those are bad, bad girls," Roseanne replied with certainty, looking straight ahead.

"Why, Roseanne, why are the girls bad? What did they do?" Had they teased her or even pushed her around? Had they tried to get her to do something? Were they stealing from each other?

"Drugs," she answered, eyes on the ceiling and one finger pointing. "They were doing drugs." Jeanne was flabbergasted. What a terrible revelation. It was an awful shock to hear that girls were actually doing drugs during school in the locker room. There would be student expulsions, maybe even incarceration.

Drugs were simply not allowed in school, and there were no protections for students who were not classified. Even if a student was classified and protected as a special education student, a manifestation determination would have to be conducted. A team would determine if the behavior had a relationship to the handicap. In drug cases that would be difficult to prove. The girls in the gym class were not classified. Most likely they would be permanently expelled from high school.

Not only that, but teachers would get fired. They should have been aware of what was going on in the locker room.

Worse still, this would get around the high school in a flash. The kids in the special education classroom would be branded as narks forever. What a tragedy—they would be shunned, picked on, and persecuted. Jeanne would have to report that students had drugs in school, and Kathy would probably be fired for sure. "Oh, Roseanne, are you sure?" she asked.

"Yep, they are doing drugs."

Jeanne just did not want to believe it—what an awful mess. She decided she had better be very sure about every detail before letting this bomb drop. "What drugs, Roseanne?"

"Cocaine," she answered, struggling to pronounce the word.

"Where, where were they doing cocaine?"

"In the locker room."

"Where was the teacher? Did she see them doing cocaine?"

"No," Roseanne answered shaking her head back and forth too hard. "The teacher was in her office."

Jeanne still could not believe this. What could she do to defuse this situation? Nothing, not a thing. "Roseanne," she said, staring intently at her. "What does cocaine look like?"

"It's white powder," she replied with absolute knowledge and more certain about that than she was about how to spell her last name.

Jeanne rose to take Roseanne back to class and then walk down a long flight of stairs to the principal's office. She had no choice but to alert others in the administration. This was always difficult. Young people are permanently expelled from school. The consequences are lifelong.

"Roseanne," she said, prompted to probe further, to find out all the details, by what had happened to Alex. Due process is not jumping to conclusions until every aspect of a situation has been explored. This is critical when students with special needs are concerned. Jeanne asked one more question. "What did the girls do with the white powder?"

Roseanne turned and explained in her very certain voice, "They put it under their arms and on their backs."

Jeanne almost fell over with surprise. "Like this?" she mimed shaking baby powder out of a jar and putting it on her underarms.

"Yes, that's what they did."

Jeanne grabbed Roseanne and hugged her. "Yes!" she shouted right in the hallway. She ran into Danna's classroom and explained what Roseanne had actually seen, thankful for the lessons from Alex.

Kathy and Danna had a good laugh about the white powder. They showed Roseanne what it was so she understood the girls were not doing drugs. Kathy decided to walk around the locker room more. It is a delicate balance since teachers don't want to watch girls shower or get dressed, but they need to be a presence while students are there.

Roseanne continued to attend the P.E. class without any problems. She never wanted to use baby powder under her arms, but she did listen to what the high school girls said. Kathy felt that much of the catty remarks and teasing often heard in locker rooms had diminished. The girls were protective of someone with disabilities and started being more thoughtful to each other, too.

The psychiatric report indicated that Alex was a young man possibly older than his stated age. He was functioning normally, alert to time and place. He was eager to make new friends and concerned about fitting in at his new school. His intelligence was low-average, putting him at risk to be manipulated by others. There were no areas of concern.

The diagnostic team met and determined that his behavior, although totally inappropriate, was related to his learning disability. It was difficult for him to process social interactions accurately. He would need special instruction and support from his teachers to learn appropriate responses when other students were teasing him. They recommended that he return to the middle school. The days of suspension he had already served were punishment enough.

Jennifer met with the entire middle school faculty about teasing and what could be done to stop it. Alex returned to the middle school without any incident. Sadly, his father died suddenly just before the summer vacation. The family moved away and Alex never returned to the district. Due process, however, has been around for eight hundred years and will hopefully be around for at least eight hundred more.

ESSENTIAL UNDERSTANDINGS

- This chapter illustrates how the deficit approach for individuals with mild intellectual disabilities (ID) limits their potential. When individuals are defined by a category, other strengths are ignored.
- Many individuals with ID have physical, artistic, and musical skills, yet IDEA classifications are based on a medical model that is focused on the problems and basically ignores strengths. This was helpful in gaining sympathy and funding for programs; however, along with the curriculum, this view of individuals with disabilities needs to change.
- Exposure to different situations that challenge them are an important part of the educational experience for students with disabilities, their peers, and their teachers.
- When a student who has a disability and is protected by the IDEA breaks a school rule, a team of special education professionals who are knowledgeable about the student must meet and review the student's individualized education program. If the IEP is appropriate and being properly implemented, then the team could determine if the student's behavior was caused by, or related to, their handicapping condition. This is called a manifestation determination. This team can decide if the educational placement needs to be changed.
- A building principal, the superintendent, or even the members of the school board cannot expel a student with special needs from school without due process. For example bringing alcohol to school is illegal, but in Roseanne's case the incident was clearly related to her disability. She thought it was a can of soda. The determination was made by the district diagnostic team.
- Teachers are responsible for student safety and are legally liable if they are negligent and something happens to a child. They need to be aware of everything that is going on in the classroom. If a teacher was on the phone and their student got injured, it would be criminal negligence.
- The IEP is not a flexible document. The IDEA does not allow teachers to experiment with a program change to see if it might be better. An IEP is written for an entire school year, not for a week.

- A meeting to change an existing IEP would require a special education teacher, a general education teacher, the case manager, a school administrator, parents, and the student, if the student is older than fourteen. That kind of a meeting might take weeks to schedule. Experimentation is not part of the rigid rules of the IDEA.

SIX

===

Intruder

There are many ways to get out of a school building, but only one or two ways to get in. Access is carefully monitored with locked doors and an intercom system or guards stationed just inside. Visitors must sign in and out, noting the time they arrive and when they leave. The staff, and even the students in some schools, wear badges. Children are carefully taught that they must never, ever, open a door for anyone. Not even their own grandmother.

Teachers, supervisors, principals, custodians, and lunch ladies have been trained, sometimes by Israeli soldiers, on how to respond to intruders. Safe spaces have been identified. In case of a bomb threat, teachers and custodians scan the areas they know to see if anything extra has been placed there. They look to see if anything has been moved. Teachers and students have practiced fire drills for decades. Everyone quietly leaves the building while a bell rings so loudly you are eager to get outside.

Once students were evacuated from a school in dangerous situations, but we learned that shooters or bombs could be waiting outside as the children emerge from the building. Today, lockdown drills are in place. Teachers know the codes that indicate danger and quickly gather children behind locked doors and away from windows.

The school secretaries have a list on their desk regarding a bomb threat. They listen very carefully and may try to engage the caller in a conversation. They estimate the age of the caller, the sex, any background sounds, and any accent.

The school nurses, psychologists, social workers, and counselors form emergency response teams at the beginning of the year. They are ready to drop everything and quickly mobilize to any school where a traumatic event has taken place. They can set up counseling stations in a school often within fifteen minutes. The unexpected death of a child or a teacher triggers a fast response.

Administrators have been trained in what to do during emotional situations for students. Supervisors and teachers know that a normal school day should continue as much as possible. They do not broadcast the event over a loudspeaker. Teachers are quickly informed factually about what happened and they quietly inform their students during class. Administrators insist that students go to class and do not allow them to roam the hallways or leave the building. They do not want hysterical children roaming outside the school. Some students are impacted by the event, others don't process it until later. Everyone needs the security of routine.

Counselors who know the children are available in special areas throughout the school and teachers urge all students who are upset to go to a station and seek out a counselor. Those students who are not upset at one moment may become so later. The counseling may continue throughout the day and into the evening for families over several days.

Despite all of this training and preparation, intruders somehow still manage to evade all of the precautions and get into school buildings.

Wheat School is an old brick building set securely in a tightly knit neighborhood. Most of the parents attended this very school, and mothers gather outside in the morning and afternoon to pick up their children. They discuss Avon nail polish and the school gift-wrap sale. The building is the oldest working school in New Jersey and was designed with doors in every hallway so the children could get out quickly in case of a fire. *Boys* is chiseled in the stone over one doorway. The girl's entrance is on the other side of the building and is now used by the kindergarten.

An electronic door release and camera were installed at the front door. These days all the outside-access doors are locked. After the children come inside each morning, the only way to get inside is through the front door. A security camera records everything. The school secretary and the principal have been trained in security detail. Joanne, the secretary, checks the video monitor and buzzes familiar people inside. Everyone must report to the office, sign in, and wear a large pass to indicate that they are legally allowed in the building.

The children are taught not to open doors in any circumstance, for anyone. They would march right past their own mother holding birthday cupcakes—at least that is what everyone thought. Everyone, including the Jeanne, the director of special services, had to ring the bell at the front door and wait to be recognized.

Despite all of the elaborate electronic security precautions, an intruder managed to evade the entire system at the Wheat Elementary School. That morning, a cluster of children on their way to the library stalled by the outside-access door at the side of the building.

Jeanne saw the group of children as she hurried down the stairs on her way to the basement lunchroom where English as a second language (ESL) classes were held. Something had impeded the children's trip down the stairs to the library in the basement. When she stopped to investigate why so many children were gathered in front of the side door, the second graders looked up with guilty glances. They had surrounded a very happy dog. His tail was wagging and his tongue was licking everyone he could reach as they bent down to pet him.

One boy with round brown eyes and a Spider-Man bandage on his forehead bit his lower lip and watched her carefully. Perhaps this was the one who had opened the outside door and let the dog in.

Years ago a teacher offered the student who earned the most points for good behavior an opportunity to go home with her after school and cuddle with her fluffy golden retriever. There are people alive today who were saved from illiteracy by the competition to go home with their teacher and play with that dog. A snuggle in school these days, unthinkable!

The administrative team had completed emergency management plans to handle bomb threats, chemical spills, kidnapping, plane crashes, shootings and stabbings, floods, power failure, and flooding. Teachers have gone beyond fire drills to lockdowns. They know to lock the door and stay away from the windows when there is a code blue and an intruder has been spotted in the building. All of these plans have been monitored by the county office and shared with the police. The nurse has a crisis cart with medication and emergency equipment ready to roll at any time. However, someone had defied all the rules and now six seven-year-old children were hugging and kissing an intruder despite all the best efforts to protect them.

It was a happy little scene and Jeanne paused for a moment to enjoy the children's delight at their exciting little secret. A dog in school! A few minutes passed and their second-grade teacher sent a child to see what had happened to the rest of her students. The messenger came up the steps, saw the dog, and instantly knelt down in awe. He mumbled, "Miss Shine says you have to go to the library," with his cheek nuzzled into the furry neck.

The children hesitated. Several hugged the dog desperately, looking up with beseeching eyes. "What a good doggie" they wailed. "Can't he stay here today?"

Jeanne couldn't resist and asked, "Is this a new student?" The dog wagged his tail slowly, softening her up. The children smiled; a game was afoot. "Do you want to come to school here?" she asked the spotted invader in her most adult tone.

"Oh yes! Oh yes he does!" The children shouted, hoping against all odds that maybe the dog could come to school.

"We shall have to find out what class to put you in then," she continued. "Do you know how to count to twenty-five?" A tail wagged. "Hmm. What does this spell: D O G?" The four-legged applicant looked up expectantly, and licked his shiny black nose. "I can't put you in second grade if you can't count," Jeanne warned, smiling. Some children started to understand the probable outcome of this interrogation. They understood that the dog would not be attending their class. Several other children proudly shared that they could count all the way to one hundred.

"What color is your coat?" Jeanne pointed her finger at the dog and it sat down and offered his paw. The children were all shrieking with delight. "No, that's not the right answer either," Jeanne said, shaking her head from side to side to the continued laughter of the children. "I'm sorry," she said. "If you don't know your colors or how to count, you can't come to school."

Just then footsteps stopped above and Mr. Williams, the principal, appeared at the top of the stairs. Nothing goes on in schools for long before the principal knows about it. He leaned over the children and pushed open the door for the dog without further ado. The game was over and Spot left without a whimper, totting off into the windy day, tail flying.

The children lingered a moment around Mr. Williams. Several wanted to share something about the dog with him, "Mr. W., Mr. W.! We got a puppy but my mother says if she whines all night again we'll have to take her back." Every single child touched this man as they passed by. Some just brushed a finger on the back of his jacket, but everyone wanted some sort of contact.

It was reminiscent of when the Torah is taken out of the Ark during services in a Jewish synagogue. The rabbi walks up and down the aisles while reverent hands touch the holy book of the law with their prayer book or prayer shawl as it is carried by. The Bible and the Koran are treated as reverently. In schools, the building principal embodies the set of rules that ensure we are kind to others, and they are kind to us. The children were disappointed that the dog couldn't stay in school, but they love the person who brings safety and security in this troubled world. Plans and electronics are important, but they will never replace careful attention to people.

ESSENTIAL UNDERSTANDING

- School administrators have installed elaborate alarm systems to ensure student safety. A four-legged intruder did manage to sneak inside a school, much to the delight of the second graders, but nothing gets past a good principal.

SEVEN

They Don't Belong Here

The treatment of disabled students should be a source of national shame: They represent 12 percent of students in the country, but they make up 25 percent of students receiving multiple out-of-school suspensions and 23 percent of students subjected to a school-related arrest.
— The Department of Education Office for Civil Rights

The first day of school can be wonderful, and it can be a disaster. Parents stand in little family groups on the lawn and sidewalks around the school. They straighten hair bows and tuck in new shirts. The boys have fresh haircuts. Fathers make movies and mothers take pictures, but the children are oblivious. They are shouting at friends and eager to get inside.

A few children cry. One little boy reported, "My eyes are leaking, I don't know why." His mother twisted her ring and shifted from foot to foot as if she could still rock her baby. It is the end of the summer, and parents are both sad and grateful. They will now be able to linger in the supermarket or clean the kitchen floor without interruption.

The teachers have forgotten whatever little snits they had with each other in June. Mortal enemies greet each other with a hug and air kisses in the halls. Rooms smell nice, the crayons are new, and glue bottles are full. Unlike any other job, teachers get to do everything all over again. This year they will get it right. After five years of teaching fourth grade, they have a better understanding of what works and what does not. This year, students will be asked to help write the classroom rules. They will not teach fractions until everyone understands decimals. This year they will do that lesson on contractions first, then continue with possessives.

There is nothing quite like that new beginning. New shoes squeak on the waxed floors as the children file in, all smiles and all happy. Today they are on their best behavior. Anxious groups of mothers linger near their cars talking, but all eyes are on the school. If they could peek into the windows they would. However, parents know they cannot cross the threshold—they go home leaving the teachers to start a fresh new year. It is much better than New Year's Eve.

On the first day of school plans that have been worked on all summer can go terribly wrong. When Jeanne, the director of special services, walked into her office that bright September day, her secretary had that look on her face. There was trouble. "Well, he didn't last five minutes," she announced.

"Who?"

"Leo, that new kid with autism that you put in fifth grade. They threw him out of school, he's already home."

"Good God! It's not even nine o'clock. What happened?"

"The very first thing he did was to punch a poor kid on crutches and knock him over."

Jeanne turned and got right back in her car to drive over to the school. Leo had a lot of energy and he didn't sit still—but he was not vicious. She could only imagine what had happened. Those teachers were just not going to have a child with autism in their classes, she thought. Jeanne had heard those sentiments at every single meeting about putting Leo into a general education classroom. She had ended up saying, "It's the law," knowing that the law is just a piece of paper written in Washington, DC, and that is a long way from the fifth grade.

Jeanne parked in the fire lane at the school and stormed up the steps. Inside the door, she thought she had better take some deep breaths or risk saying something that would make the situation worse. The building principal, Daniel, was coming down the hall and greeted her with "Let's talk in my office."

Jeanne could sense that he was also angry. Everyone tried to have a smooth opening, a good start to the school year. Suspending a student on the first day was very upsetting. "Jeanne," he started, "Leo needs to be in a special school. He does not belong here, as I told you repeatedly all summer."

"Daniel, just tell me what happened," she interrupted him.

"One of the fifth graders in Leo's room was in a baseball accident this summer, and he broke his leg in three places. He came to school today in a full leg cast and on crutches. We had the nurse walk behind him in the halls until she was sure that he was competent on the crutches and would not fall and hurt himself. He was doing just fine, and she let him go into the classroom.

"The boy walked into the classroom and stood at the front of the room talking to the teacher. Leo got up out of his seat and ran over and started swearing at him, 'Jesus Christ! Jesus Christ!' he shouted. Then before anyone could stop him, Leo pushed the kid right over on the floor. He put both hands on the kid's chest and pushed hard."

Jeanne was stunned. So it was true. Leo had attacked another student. Why hadn't anyone at his previous school told her about this behavior? Sometimes schools are eager to get rid of difficult students (or parents) and don't reveal everything they should. She was furious at his special education school, his parents, and herself.

Daniel continued before she could start apologizing. "This was no accident, Leo knew exactly what he was doing and he did it on purpose! He even looked at his aide and smiled afterward as though he was proud of himself. It was terrible. What kind of a monster does that? He does not belong in this school, Jeanne. I will go the board of education and fight this placement as long as I have to, I'll tell you that."

Daniel was puffing at this point and his ears were red. Jeanne had never seen him so angry. She collapsed in a chair. "Daniel, calm down," she said. "I can't believe this—it is terrible. Was that poor boy hurt?"

"No, thankfully he was not hurt, but his parents are pretty upset about this. Parents in this building are not going to tolerate these special education students attacking other kids. Children with autism don't belong in a regular school. Jeanne, how many times do I have to say this?"

"Daniel, parents don't dictate who is and isn't in our classes, we do. Legally, kids with special needs have a right to attend the same school as other children unless they are a danger to themselves or others. Daniel, this is a total shock. Leo has never, ever done anything like this at all. I am so sorry about this. I can't understand why he would push another child to the ground."

Both administrators took a deep breath and felt calmer. There was no reason to attack each other; it would only make the problem worse. In a moment of silence after the angry exchange, the ticking of the old wooden clock on the wall over Daniel's desk was audible. Who knew clocks ticked so loudly?

"Leo's mother picked him up and he's at home. Maybe she will listen to reason now," Daniel said. They both remembered the five tense meetings they had had with her over the summer. She was a determined woman, and she had an answer for every concern that had been presented. Leo had a legal right to be in his neighborhood school under the least restrictive placement requirement of the Individuals with Disabilities Education Act (IDEA).

Due to her firm insistence, Jeanne and Daniel had relented and agreed to include Leo in the fifth grade. Jeanne had hired an individual aide for him who was experienced with students on the autism spectrum. She set up training sessions for the classroom teacher about children with autism.

Daniel had scheduled an in-service training session for the entire faculty on the first open day. This training could not be scheduled before the start of the school year. Teachers have a specific 185-day contract, and they could not be compelled to come in during the summer unless they were paid. Even then, it had to be optional. Jeanne didn't think any of the training would have prepared the teachers for Leo going crazy and punching a helpless child on crutches.

Leo had been diagnosed with autism when he was only three years old. Autism is a spectrum disorder, which means that it encompasses a wide variety of abilities and challenges. Children with autism spectrum disorder can be low functioning, nonverbal, preoccupied with a few objects, and some exhibit aggressive behaviors. Others can function independently, have good intellectual abilities, and initiate social interactions.

The Individuals with Disabilities Education Act of 1990 identifies characteristics of autism as engagement in repetitive activities, stereotyped movements, resistance to change or routines, and unusual responses to sensory experiences. Many of the characteristics associated with autism spectrum disorder, or ASD, fall into three core deficit areas: (1) communication (2) socialization and (3) repetitive interests and behaviors.

Most individuals diagnosed on the autism spectrum have behavioral deficits. These typically include an inability to relate to others, lack of functional language, sensory processing deficits, and cognitive deficits. Problem behaviors may include noncompliance, perseverative actions, and aggressive behaviors such as spitting, biting, or hitting. Unfortunately, some children display self-injurious actions such a biting their hand, hair pulling, or head-banging. People with autism often become easily overaroused in situations that are stressful to them and, once overstimulated, they remain so for extended periods.

Although he had been diagnosed on the autism spectrum, Leo had never been aggressive. His former school had not reported any instance where he had attacked someone. If anything, Leo had been sheltered and protected by his mother. He was an only child, and she had fed him until he was four and still waited on him hand and foot. She chose his clothes and dressed him each morning.

Children, even those with autism, don't just snap and become violent all of a sudden. They could punch back when threatened and will learn how to hit and pinch from watching others, but there is always a reason for their behavior. Swearing and pushing someone over for no reason was incomprehensible. It would inflame the misconceptions about individuals with disabilities.

Jeanne considered driving over to Leo's home to speak with his mother, but decided that everybody needed to be allowed to calm down and consider what had happened very carefully. Time and distance would help that process. This new idea of placing a child with autism in a regular fifth-grade class had been a disaster despite weeks of careful planning.

School administrators do not have the months of July and August free. Most work a twelve-month year; most administrative pay scales don't compensate them for this. Hour for hour a comparison of administrators and teachers reveals most principals and directors work for less than teachers do.

Summer does bring some relief from day-to-day issues. All the doors to the classrooms are open, and the smells of chlorine bleach and pine embrace you when you walk into the building. Security systems are turned off. The precious charges have run off to the community pool where they are watched by lifeguards and slathered in sunblock.

The classrooms are mostly empty; however, the detritus of human behavior is everywhere. Chairs and tables are stacked in the hall so the classroom floors can at last be really cleaned. Those dreadful pictures of butterflies that all looked alike have been taken down from the bulletin board outside the library. There are one or two summer classes, a special art club, and the friendship group. Directors can linger over coffee with the principal. They talk about their own children.

This languid pace is really only a chimera. There are a lot of things to accomplish and only five weeks before the band begins to practice in the parking lot behind the administration building. They march back and forth, turning and running into each other, playing one song over and over. Thinking must be done in July.

During the last week of school, Jeanne met with the members of the child study team frequently to review unsolved problems. The case managers for the students alerted her to any issues that had not been resolved. Programs and placements would have to be found during the summer. Every single child needed a place to go, a classroom and a teacher on the first day of school. Finding teachers and places would be the director's responsibility during the summer months.

Jeanne had been told that Leonardo Lothario's mother was not happy with his program. Leo attended a private school for children with autism and had always been in special schools. Leo's mother felt that the special education schools had done very little to help her son. He was a high-functioning child who could read at a second-grade level. He had a large reading vocabulary, but struggled with comprehension. His best subject was math. He loved trains and train schedules. After saying hello to someone, he would usually begin to talk about trains in a monotone. He talked quickly, and without pausing, about this favorite subject.

Despite these skills, Leo had been placed in a class at the private school with some nonverbal children. The school felt that this class was the most appropriate placement for him. His school specialized in children with autism and had a one to one staff to student ratio. The school had a pool, a farm, and even a supermarket for the older students to practice vocational skills.

Each year at an annual review meeting, parents are presented with the individualized education program (IEP) proposed for their child for the following year. Mrs. Lothario had refused to agree to continue Leo's placement at the private school for students with autism. She would not allow her son to return in the fall and wanted another program.

Mrs. Lothario felt that his obsessive talk about trains might diminish if other children responded to him in a normal way. She felt he needed to be challenged academically more than he was in the special school. She wanted him to be included with neurotypical children his own age. She wanted the children in the neighborhood to get to know her son. Leo had never been to a birthday party.

During the spring, Leo's case manager, Rose, had taken Mrs. Lothario to visit several other schools that specialized in programs for students on the autism spectrum. They were within an hour's drive of her home. The only one she liked would not accept Leo due to his limited ability levels. She insisted that he should attend the elementary school in her neighborhood.

Children with severe disabilities are eligible for an extended school year program so they will not lose skills they learned during the school year. Most of the private schools for children with disabilities offered a summer program, and Leo attended the summer session at his special school. In late June, Jeanne decided she would go and observe Leo in his current school to get a better idea of his skills and any behavior problems. That would give her a better idea of what a possible program for him might be.

She found Leo's file and called his mother based on the contact information on the first page of the IEP. Mrs. Lothario answered and cheerfully explained that this was not an interruption. She had been cleaning out her silverware drawer. Jeanne told Mrs. Lothario that she would be visiting Leo in his summer program. She wanted to see what could be done at his private school so he could be with other students who could speak and interact with each other.

"Oh, no that is not at all what I am interested in for Leo," his mother replied. "I don't think they challenge him there at all. He can read and he never gets any homework. He can add, subtract, multiply, and divide. He talks his head off at home, and he has a gerbil that he takes care of all by himself. I don't think that school is right for my son. He needs to be challenged or he doesn't do anything."

"I will talk to them about putting together a more academic program for him."

"No, I'm telling you, I have been all over them every year he has been there—they don't believe in reading difficult books, they just want him to stack cans when he grows up. That is all they think he can do." Mrs. Lothario was a fast talker; words flowed out of her mouth without a breath. "I want him to attend his neighborhood school. He needs to know the children in our neighborhood; he needs to learn how to get along with them. He is going to live here when he grows up; he needs to learn about his own town."

"Mrs. Lothario, I don't have a program for someone on the autism spectrum at that school. At this point we only have an autism class for the preschool children. We just don't have the right program for him here in town."

She barely let Jeanne finish the sentence, "I know all that, I have heard all that before. I don't want him with those kids in special schools. I want him in fifth grade, he's ten and that is where he belongs."

This was exactly what Rose, Leo's case manager had described. Mrs. Lothario had been reading about "inclusion," where children with autism and other developmental disabilities attend classes with normally developing children. It was hard for Jeanne to consider this new idea called the regular education initiative. She wondered what people in Washington, DC, knew about children with special needs.

Special educators had worked long and hard to develop classes and special programs that would protect children with disabilities. It was hurtful to have them rejected in favor of general education classes. It was horrifying actually. Special education teachers assumed that children would make fun of special education students. The special child would sit in the back of the room and maybe color while the rest of the class studied the metamorphosis of the spotted salamander.

The special self-contained classes were created to be at their learning level and to engage them in academic activities in which they would be successful. If a special student was not doing well, the curriculum would be modified. This was not going to happen in a general education class. The teacher would move on to the next topic, rather than hold the entire class back. Why would any parent want to subject their child to potential failure in programs not designed specifically for their special child?

The school Leo attended had speech therapists, physical therapists, and occupational therapists there every day with special equipment. All of the teachers including the gym and art faculty wanted to work with handicapped children. Almost none of the teachers in the public schools wanted to work with handicapped children. They didn't want them in the halls or even the lunchroom with the other children—they certainly didn't want them in their classrooms.

"I am determined that this will happen in September," Leo's mother continued. "I am praying about this every day. I know my rights to have him placed in the least restrictive environment, and I intend to make sure it will happen."

She was absolutely correct. Federal and state laws such as the IDEA required that students with special needs attend classes with normally developing students (the least restrictive environment) whenever possible. Districts were legally required to do everything within reason to allow this to happen. Instructional aides, teacher training, counseling, busing, and other supports had to be in place in order for this to be successful. Interventions even included medical services as long as they did not require a doctor to perform them. Only when the special student disrupted the classroom despite the interventions were districts allowed to force the child to attend a special education program.

Jeanne interrupted to buy some time. She still hoped to dissuade Mrs. Lothario from her request. "Well, let me go and see him. I think I should know more about Leo than what is written in his test reports and IEP." This seemed to appease his mother; however, she remained convinced of the logic of her request. Jeanne thought there was no way that this could happen. There was not one single general education teacher at his school who would be happy to have a student with autism in their classroom.

Leo's school principal made an appointment for Jeanne to come and observe the school in early July. The fifty-minute drive was peaceful. She turned off the highway and down a two-lane road through cornfields and blinking yellow lights. The school was located in an old convent. Its small sign was partially hidden in blue chicory that grew tall along the roadside.

The principal had warned Jeanne that she had gone too far if she came to a stop sign and a stone fence. A red-winged blackbird posed on last year's cattails when she turned the car around. The long gravel drive curled around the old stone buildings. Parking was in a level field next to the main building. Several other buildings could be reached by cement walks and a covered portico led from the main school building down to a ramp on the drive marked "buses only."

Jeanne read through several of the full color brochures that described the program and the services offered at the special school for children with autism. Applied behavior analysis (ABA), speech therapy, physical therapy, swimming, and vocational training were described along with pictures of children and teachers. Some of the children were wearing helmets. There were no laboriously colored drawings of flowers or bumblebees lining the halls. There were pictures of the founder and major donors at fund-raising events from the last few years. Susan, the assistant principal, greeted her after a short wait in the central office.

Susan apologized that she had a meeting during a brief tour of the facilities and could not linger. She assured Jeanne that Leo had been placed in their most appropriate class for a child with his disability. She also admitted that he was already in the class with the most advanced students at the school.

The classrooms were bright and about half the size of those in public schools. Each class had five to eight students, a teacher and one instructional aide for every child. The cafeteria was built so that students in wheelchairs could see what was offered for lunch. The gym was small and had a basket low enough for a child in a wheelchair to manage. One wall had mats and supports in colorful plastic and myriad shapes.

Susan pointed out the time-out room. It was a small room with a big window, a soft rug and a single chair. The crisis intervention counselor was inside with a student. The reluctant child was curled right under the chair and hanging on to one leg. The counselor must have been six feet tall with a head of blonde curly hair. He remained patient and calm despite the provocation of the wailing, kicking child. Jeanne was impressed. Sometimes children needed a safe place and a safe person to calm down. They did not need to be yelled at when they were upset about something. Crisis counselors and special rooms were unavailable in public schools.

Susan pointed out the swimming pool, the vocational shop building, and a small fenced barnyard where chickens, a goat, and a donkey lived. They were cared for by the children. She stopped in front of Leo's classroom and introduced Jeanne to his teacher. She was working with one child at a small table while instructional aides worked with other children in small booths. Susan pointed out that several of the aides were fully certified teachers. They were recent graduates and took positions in special schools to get experience.

Jeanne sat in one of the small chairs to watch for a while. None of the children looked up to see who had come in the door except for Leo who stared intently from the back corner where he was sitting. He had earphones on, but it did not seem that whatever he had been listening too was playing anymore. A child opened the bathroom door and walked out into the classroom with his pants around his knees. An aide got up and helped him to pull up his pants and zip the fly.

A physical therapist came into the room and took a small girl with pink tape on her helmet out to her therapy session. Leo lay across the desk, his arms flopping to the other side then started to lean back in his chair back and forth each time a little further back. The chair had tennis balls on its legs.

Jeanne tried not to appear to be staring at him in case her presence in the room was encouraging his behavior, but she noticed he had his eyes on the teacher the entire time he rocked. In the middle of a backward lean that seemed ripe for disaster, his teacher noticed and got up and went over to Leo and straightened his chair. She adjusted the audiotape at that point and watched from behind as he put his elbows on the table and rested his chin on his palms while listening. He did not have a book so that he could read along with the story.

When his teacher went back to her seat, Leo's eyes followed her and he had a satisfied little smile on his face. He had short, dark hair and eyes that switched from confused to mischievous every five seconds. He was large for ten and pudgy with round cheeks and a growing belly. It didn't appear that he went outside after school to ride his bike or play baseball.

Fascinating as Leo was, one of the aides and the teacher were equally curious. They were aware of the observer in the room and who she was. Even so, they continued a conversation that seemed to have been going on for a while. The aide was young and quite pretty. She was probably a recent graduate or even a summer worker. She had long, black hair tucked behind her ears.

She was prompting her student to stack three boxes one on top of the other. She was using the hand over hand technique and would take his hand in hers and use it to stack the three boxes. "Now you do it," she repeated after they had stacked three boxes together. He pulled his arm away and stared vacantly off into the distance. She retrieved his hand and they stacked the boxes together again. They were using small cereal boxes of Cheerios and Corn Flakes. Again and again she stacked, and he passively let her guide his hand. He never looked at her or at the boxes.

During this activity she carried on a conversation with the teacher about a local restaurant. Jeanne assumed that the teacher would soon instruct the aide to switch to another task that might interest the student.

Finally, the aide got up to greet a child who was returning from speech therapy. She and the therapist also spent several minutes talking about the same restaurant. This seemed a waste of time; however, it was the stacking student who surprised Jeanne.

As soon as the aide got up and walked away, he picked up the Cheerios box. He used a slender finger to run under the little tab that keeps the box closed. He opened the box and proceeded to roll open the waxed paper lining. Then he carefully checked the inside of the box for Cheerios. He didn't find any and proceeded to open the other two boxes. They were both empty as well, and he took a big stretch with hands high above his head and slumped back into the chair, shoulders down, looking at nothing.

Jeanne thanked the teacher for her time and took the long way back to the district. She didn't stop for lunch at the restaurant they discussed. She had a problem to think about. If a student in a public school came out of the bathroom with his pants down, everyone would go crazy. The teacher and aide would hurry him back into the bathroom. A plan would be put into place so it never happened again. Training, cues, rewards, more supervision would be considered and tried. There would be an urgency about basic socialization that had been missing in the special program.

She wondered what culture prevailed in this private school that gave the faculty tacit approval to continue with a task over and over when it was obviously not interesting to the student. It felt oddly familiar and Jeanne remembered her work in the institutions for the mentally retarded. It reminded her of Edward who lived at the Belchertown State Institution for the Feeble-Minded. He refused to walk, and the staff dragged him to the cafeteria day after day. As a program coordinator for the newly established Bureau of Institutional Schools, she had ordered a physical therapy consult as part of the evaluation mandated by the IDEA.

The physical therapist (P.T.) reported that his therapeutic shoes were too small and obviously hurt his feet. The staff had been jamming his feet into shoes that were much too small for him. No wonder he would not walk! When confronted, the staff nurse retorted that he had to wear his special orthopedic shoes and the hospital could not afford another pair. Trapped between a child's growing foot and a doctor's orders for orthopedic shoes, she had followed the orders and ignored the child.

Now here was Leo in a special school where some of the teachers did not seem to feel any special urgency about what they were doing with children. The aide was following a prescribed program, but nothing was modified when the child was not responding to it.

When Jeanne got back to her office, she checked the budget figures and mused that Leo's tuition at the private school was seventy-five thousand dollars a year plus another ten thousand for the summer program. The school district paid an additional fee for the occupational therapist required in Leo's IEP. The bus to transport Leo back and forth fifty miles each way was about twenty thousand dollars. This special program was more than 100,000 dollars a year! Could that money be used in district to provide a better program for him in his neighborhood school?

It was a complicated problem. In this small school district there simply were no other children Leo's age with autism, with whom to form a self-contained class. Even if the district put a class together and had a room for it, parent approval was necessary in order to change a child's placement.

Most parents of children with autism were content with their child's special school placement. They did not mind the long commutes to and from the private schools as long as the children were safe and well cared for. They liked the extended school program in the summer, the specifically trained dedicated teachers, the related services, and the swimming pools. There were special parent groups and supportive lectures. Most special education schools had vocational programs and could keep students until they were twenty-one years old and no longer eligible for school district funding.

Under state and federal laws, children with disabilities can be grouped in classes with a three-year age span from the youngest child to the oldest. Jeanne tried to see if Leo could attend the high school special class program, but he was several years too young. He was too old to attend the special class for preschool children even though some of those students would be six in the fall.

One possibility remained. There was a self-contained class for children with learning disabilities at the middle school. At ten, Leo was within the three-year age range of the children in that class. The teacher of that self-contained class was not happy working there and had requested a transfer to an open position in an elementary resource center class for children with minor disabilities.

Jeanne had interviewed an applicant who had experience with students on the autism spectrum as well as students with learning disabilities. She might be able to handle a boy on the autism spectrum along with the other children in the class. Jeanne decided to make the transfer and hire another teacher for the middle school self-contained program.

Even though the self-contained class was housed in the middle school, most of the students stayed with the special education teacher all day. Some of the more advanced students joined regular classes where they were able to manage the regular curriculum. Leo could stay in the special class all day until he was comfortable with the routine of the school. His teacher could determine if he could attend some regular classes at the middle school. She would know the teachers and would find one interested in working with Leo. This could all happen gradually in a well-controlled manner.

Administrators are required to talk to a reference for any teacher they planned to ask the superintendent to hire. No administrator can be in the classroom all the time with teachers, however, young defenseless children are under their control. It is essential that people were hired who would be appropriate with the children no matter what provocation happened.

Jeanne dialed the number of the teacher's reference but the phone rang and rang. She wondered how the office could be empty in July. What kind of a district can close entirely during the summer? Perhaps it was too early for anyone to be in the office. Jeanne didn't want to go with her second choice just because she could not get a reference on the teacher she wanted. She needed a teacher with experience in autism.

She called back later in the day and this time put the phone on speaker and let it ring while she checked the IEPs written during the last month of school for errors. Sure enough, there was a little click and the ringing stopped. However there was just panting on the other end of the line. Finally a man's voice gasped, "Sorry, give me a minute." The deep breaths continued and Jeanne wondered how far he had run to answer the phone or if he were risking a heart attack. "This is Peter Grisham, superintendent," he finally said.

"Hello, Mr. Grisham, she replied. "I am the director of special education, and I am looking for a reference on one of your staff members."

"Fine," he replied. "Give me another minute to catch my breath. The custodial staff is off for the month of July and so is my office staff. I was out mowing the lawn when I heard the phone ringing." Summers are difficult for administrators. Everybody is gone on vacation, and everything still needs to be done. Peter had an excellent reference for Julie, who had been commuting over an hour to get to his district. She had already resigned due to the distance. Leo's district was much closer to her home. She was an outstanding candidate to present to the board of education as a new middle school teacher in the special education class.

Jeanne was eager to call Mrs. Lothario and tell her she would be able to put Leo in the special education class at the middle school. She would hire an additional aide for the class with the money saved from his tuition. An occupational therapist would be hired to provide his therapy. His new special education teacher even had experience with students with autism.

Mrs. Lothario was brusque on the telephone. "No, I am not interested in any more special education classes in our district or anywhere else," she said. Finality rang in her every word. "I want my child to be included in his fifth grade in the elementary school in my neighborhood. He deserves that, he is a person with rights, and I know them."

"I don't know how he could possibly cope with a fifth-grade class," Jeanne sputtered. What she was not saying, but hoping that Leo's mother would somehow hear, was that the fifth-grade teachers were not interested in special education children. Not at all. They saw their job as preparing children to enter the middle school in sixth grade, and they were, each one of them, quite demanding both academically and behaviorally. Children who had no problems other than a little lisp struggled through that fifth-grade year. Usually the sixth grade was much easier, and children who suffered in fifth grade did just fine if they could get into middle school.

Finally Jeanne put out her final gambit. "I will set up a meeting with the principal to talk about this," she said sternly. She hoped that perhaps Daniel Ethan's hawk-like visage and silent stare would help Leo's mother to understand that special education did not control the universe. What special education teachers wanted to do, or thought might be good for children, was often not at all what general educators thought was good for kids. A meeting with a principal who was dead set against a child with autism attending a fifth-grade class would help her to see the difficulties.

The five meetings that took place that summer had gone from bad to worse. The final one included the school district attorney, the Lotharios' attorney, and an advocate. Leo had a right to be in the least restrictive environment, and despite all their concerns, the district attorney advised that they would lose a lawsuit and they needed to accept Leo into the fifth grade. A fifth-grade teacher was present at the meetings, and she had reluctantly agreed to include Leo in her class. He would be accompanied at all times by a specially trained instructional aide.

Lenore, the aide, had worked with a student with autism before. She would meet him at the bus and sit next to him all day, everywhere he went. A second aide would provide her with breaks during the day and a thirty-minute lunch period. The teacher was promised Leo would never be unsupervised. An occupational therapist would provide thirty minutes of therapy three times a week. The speech therapist would evaluate Leo to see if he would benefit from additional therapy. He would have a case manager who would check on him frequently to monitor his progress.

On the very first day of school, at the very beginning of the day, all of these careful plans had fallen apart in an appalling way.

After her meeting with Daniel on what Leo had done in the very first minutes of school, Jeanne was discouraged, confused, and upset. Why had she failed to find out that Leo was aggressive at times? He had turned out to be physically and verbally violent, yet she had agreed to place him in a fifth-grade classroom. She had endangered seventeen other children.

She took a detour to the drive-through car wash on her way back to her office. Something about the water rushing down the outside of the car and the power brushes swirling on the windows and covering it with white soap was comforting. It is one place where a person is totally alone. A person can even scream in frustration and not be heard over the brushes and water. Jeanne emerged fortified enough to go back to her office and not run away from the entire job screaming, "Enough! What do you want from me?"

Back at her desk, she read over the messages from the morning. Some buses had been late; three students with special needs moved in and registered that morning. The district would need to get their individualized education programs from their former districts and implement them within two weeks. The preschool teacher wanted to go over field trips before the good dates at the pumpkin farm were taken by other groups. The school year had begun.

Jeanne took a call from Leo's mother, who was hysterical and crying. "I'm so sorry," she sobbed. "This is all my fault and I am so sorry. I just hope that boy was alright."

"Yes, he is fine," Jeanne responded, curious about her total change in attitude. She had half expected Leo's mother to blame the aide or the teacher for what had happened. She could complain that the teachers had not been properly trained, that someone should have known that Leo was fast and he should have been stopped.

"I take total responsibility for this, it is totally my fault," Mrs. Lothario of the pushy attorney and the demanding advocate said.

Her admission suddenly changed everything. Parents of children with disabilities face terrific battles. The truth is that nobody in schools really wants them or their children. Jeanne had not been pleased to hear that three additional children with special education needs had registered that morning.

When parents called to ask what services the district offered because they were thinking of moving in, she was not friendly or encouraging. Why would anyone try to get a parent with a difficult, expensive child to move into the district? More problems and expenses are not what teachers look for. Schools were always overwhelmed with problems.

Jeanne told Mrs. Lothario, "I don't think you are responsible for what Leo does at school."

"Oh, no, you don't understand. He was just imitating something that I showed him."

Jeanne was shocked and listened with an open mouth as Leo's mother explained. She had been very worried about how Leo would do in the elementary school. Her husband had opposed her wish that Leo attend a regular fifth grade, and they had been fighting about it. She was determined to see that her son learned everything that he could and not be held back by a lack of quality education or other children who could not talk.

"I felt this was his only chance," she resumed sobbing and told Jeanne what had happened.

She had been desperate that the fifth-grade class would work for her son. She admitted that her fight with the school had made her very anxious that Leo be successful. He was growing older, and she felt this was his last chance to be something other than autistic. She and her family talked about it all summer.

She was so worried that she had taken him to a faith healer the day before school started. The revival took place in a large tent with more than a thousand people. Mrs. Lothario sat with Leo in the front row so that he would be close to the healer. She wanted him to see and hear everything. She noted that Leo seemed quite fascinated and watched everything that happened very carefully.

After the sermon, individuals with physical problems had lined up to be touched and healed by the reverend. Many had crutches, other people were in wheelchairs. The healer had commanded the person to stand in the name of Jesus Christ, and together the crowd chanted "Jesus, Jesus."

When the person stood in front of him, the faith healer shouted "in the name of Jesus Christ" and pushed the person back into the arms of two helpers standing on either side of the person who hoped to be cured. The individual fell back into the arms of the helpers and was helped to the side of the stage, most of them in a faint.

"I kept telling him how Jesus would help him to learn in school and that he needed to remember Jesus today. Leo seemed so much better after the reverend laid his hands on him. I have so hoped for a cure!"

Suddenly Leo's behavior made sense and Jeanne could breathe again. Mrs. Lothario continued speaking as quickly as she always did. "The teacher told me what happened, and I know he saw the boy on crutches and decided to help him. Jeanne, he wasn't trying to hurt that boy, he thought he was helping."

Jeanne wanted to get off the phone so she could laugh or cry. She couldn't sit still and practically dragged the phone off of the desk pacing back and forth trying to control her voice. "Someday we will laugh about this," she said. "Hopefully we will be laughing by Christmas."

"They would not even let me explain at that school—they didn't care why Leo pushed the child. They just think he is a monster." Leo's mother was shaken by the response at the school and had experienced the rejection she had been subtly warned about all summer.

"They were pretty surprised and upset this morning. When they calm down, I will see if I can get them to understand," Jeanne assured her. However, after this experience, Leo's mother was ready to discuss placing him in the self-contained program at the middle school. He would be in the special education class for some of the day and in general classes in those areas where he would be comfortable and could benefit. A schedule would be prepared, and the district would conduct some teacher training for the general education teachers before Leo began to attend regular classes.

That very next day, Leo's mother brought him to the middle school for the orientation assembly for new students. She left him at the door in the care of his aide and his new teacher. They walked him into the auditorium. Jeanne watched from the back of the room as Leo wiggled away from his aide and teacher by crawling on the floor down the row of seats.

The aide followed him from one side while his special education teacher closed in on him from the other. One middle school student after another raised their feet up to allow Leo to crawl under them. It was amazing that none of the students in the entire row kicked or pushed Leo. They picked up their feet; he crawled under their knees. They put their feet back down, ignoring him like a pesky little brother.

Jeanne could see that they had a long way to go with Leo, but she also felt hopeful. If Leo was going to be able to go shopping with his family, eat in a restaurant, or choose books from the local library, he needed to be in his local school. As so often happens, children are better at accepting differences than adults.

ESSENTIAL UNDERSTANDINGS

- People with autism often become easily overaroused in situations that are stressful to them and, once overstimulated, they remain so for extended periods.
- Leo had always attended a special school for students with autism; however, when his mother learned about inclusion, she insisted that he be placed in a general education class in his local elementary school.
- When lawsuits about inclusion are threatened, attorneys typically advise school districts to settle and enroll the child. The IDEA has a clearly stated preference for the mainstream classroom or least restrictive environment.
- An individual aide and teacher training may not change negative attitudes in the school about students with disabilities. Attitudes

may be even more negative when teachers and administrators are compelled to include a student with special needs.

- Under state and federal laws, children with disabilities can be grouped in classes with a three-year age span from the youngest child to the oldest.
- Many parents have learned that inclusion is not a place. Inclusion is a belief, a prayer, a dance. It requires teachers to stand up to misconceptions; it requires creative thinking and an unshakable determination to find solutions to difficult problems.
- The strongest attitudes about the benefits of inclusion have evolved slowly, two steps forward and one step back. After a disastrous beginning, Leo was slowly integrated into a public school.

EIGHT

Homeless

Always do right. This will gratify some people and astonish the rest.
—Mark Twain

"There's a woman here to see you. She says she's homeless," Connie, the secretary for special services, said rolling her eyes and jerking her head in a meaningful gesture. Connie had lived in town her entire life; her father once owned the local barber shop. If you lived in town—you were family and she would do anything for you and your children. That often consisted of nagging her boss, the director of special services, to get specialized programs in place for children.

Connie was dedicated to the school district and its students. She was a force to be reckoned with if she felt a district teacher or, worse yet, an administrator was not doing a good job. If the family was new, especially immigrants from other countries, Connie considered them invaders in her special community. She felt no need to hide her contempt for a homeless person.

"Okay, I'll see her in a minute," Jeanne, the director of special services, replied sternly in an attempt to let Connie know that she would be the one making decisions about who was a legitimate student and who was not.

Kathy Baker was tall and her eyes were rimmed with red—but Jeanne didn't think it was from tears. She had a defiant look about her face and a blouse that gapped at the bust and exposed her midriff. She wore short boots with three-inch heels and a tight, ill-fitting skirt. These were the cheap gaudy clothes found in shops that catered to a certain kind of teenaged girl. Not exactly what you would wear to a meeting at a school, unless you didn't have anything else. Her voice was deep, perhaps from smoking, and when she started talking, the anxiety and trouble behind her story colored the conversation.

She had been living in a town about three miles away; however, she had been evicted and had no place to live. "I dropped my son off with my stepfather who lives up the street from here. I am living with my boyfriend," she explained.

"Jason can't live with me and my boyfriend. He can't stay home all day either, so he needs to get into school."

Kathy had been sent to see someone in special services by the elementary school principal. First she had gone to the middle school, but when she told them her son had been in a special education class, they told her to go the elementary school. Jeanne sighed at the mention of the runaround.

Nobody wanted another child with problems in their school. The district principals placed students in grades according to their age. They were not used to determining the best place for a student with special needs. It also seemed to Jeanne as if there was another, unspoken reaction: "This student doesn't belong here." The two words "homeless" and "handicapped" ensured this child would not be welcomed by either the elementary school or the middle school.

Jeanne questioned Kathy about her son. "How old is he?"

"Thirteen."

"What was his classification?"

"I don't know if anybody ever told me that."

"Do you have an IEP or any reports I can look at?"

"I had some papers but I don't know what happened to them."

"What is wrong with Jason?" Jeanne asked. It was not all that unusual for a parent to be confused by the special education jargon.

"I think they said he's retarded—he is kinda slow with school stuff. His father certainly was. He ran out on us."

"Oh dear! I am sorry to hear that," Jeanne replied. "What kind of classes did Jason attend at his last school?"

"He had a nice teacher in a small class. The other kids were retarded too."

State law mandates that all children under the age of sixteen must attend school. Public schools are required to educate any child who is a resident or domiciled within the school district. However, homeless children present a special circumstance.

Jeanne explained to Jason's mother that, as a homeless person, she had certain rights regarding her son's education. She could choose to have him continue to attend the school he had attended before becoming homeless, or he could attend the school in the district where he was staying.

Kathy looked confused and furrowed her brow. "I don't have a lot of time," she said.

"Well, let me make a suggestion," Jeanne replied. "Jason is probably upset about having to move from his home and not living with you."

"Yeah."

"It would probably be better to keep him in the school he has been attending. He knows the school and the teacher. Legally he has a right to stay in that school while you are homeless."

Convinced that this was actually the best solution in this situation, Jeanne offered more information. "A great deal in his life has changed and he was happy in his old school. Let's try to keep him there. I can call the office of special education in that district and tell them you want Jason to stay in their school. They will send a bus to pick him up so he can continue to attend classes with his teacher and the other students. Would you like me to do that?"

"Yeah, that sounds like a good idea," Kathy said; however, she still looked doubtful. She wrote down her stepfather's name and address and then she was gone. Jeanne was left with another slip of paper, another problem to do something about—or what is usually worse, getting someone else to do something about the problem.

It was easy enough to call Jason's old district and explain the situation to the secretary who answered the phone. Jeanne did her duty, but Connie snorted at the solution. "They aren't going to do anything," she said. Jeanne was aware that her secretary might be right. Jason's former home was in a large city with all of the problems that are endemic in urban districts. They have too many problems that were too big to solve with their limited resources.

"Put this in the pending file and let's check back in a week or two," Jeanne told Connie. Connie read the notes then slipped the paper into an already bulging file. Jeanne didn't know that Connie had noticed Jason wandering around in the neighborhood. He looked like a student with special needs, and she quickly discovered that he was not attending school. She had gone to the house and threatened to call the police if he was not enrolled.

All that morning the smell of home-cooked soup graced the air in the basement of the middle school where the special services offices were located. It was pasta fagioli and it was usually delicious. Homemade soup from the school cafeteria was often the highlight of the day. Lunch was a brief fifteen-minute affair for those in the special services office. They were grateful each and every day for the hot lunch program and Rosa, who managed to make tasty food from government-issued supplies. Connie answered the phones even during her lunch break. She never complained and never insisted that she should have a complete break from all of her duties. Loyal to her town and its children, she took messages and kept the office open.

"You better take this one," Connie said, holding the phone to her chest. Jeanne's soup was too hot anyway and she transferred it into her office where she had paper and could take notes. It was Mrs. Gabour saying that she wanted a copy of all of her son's records. It sounded like she was getting ready for a lawsuit. This had been brewing for a year or more. Gabriel, her son, was born with a condition that left his bones brittle and deposits of calcium grew in his skull. He was now blind, and the pressure in his skull had left him with cognitive delays.

Jeanne could never forget her very first day on the job when Mrs. Gabour called shouting that her son had come home from school with a broken leg. She was convinced that the physical therapist had broken it during a session with her child. The physical therapist had denied any wrongdoing.

It seemed this woman had something to complain about every day. The bus was late or it was early. "Is there anything wrong?" Jeanne asked.

"No, I just want all of my son's records. I will come over this afternoon and pick them up."

Parents have a right to see and have copies of all school records on their child—however they can be charged for copies. They had to be made available in a timely fashion. "We will call you when they are ready," Jeanne replied.

Mrs. Gabour was not happy, and it spilled from the corners of her mouth when she spoke. "I need those today."

"I'm sorry, we will get them copied as soon as we can and will call you by the end of the week." Jeanne knew that Connie would not be happy about making the zillion copies in Gabriel's file.

That afternoon it occurred to Jeanne that Jason's school district was working on their Individuals with Disabilities Education Act (IDEA) application for federal aid and that if they didn't get this homeless child with special needs into school by the count day, they would not be able to claim him for IDEA funding. Since he was not attending school, nobody would be able to claim this child. It was not a lot of money since the federal government had never funded the IDEA at the 40 percent level promised when the law was passed. It was only about 16 percent of the additional cost of educating a child with special needs.

The federal application needed to be submitted by Friday. Each year, every child who was classified as disabled under the IDEA, and attended school in the district, was counted. This child count was sent to Washington, DC, in an application for federal aid. The amount of money allotted to the district was based on the number of children with special needs who were attending the district on the count date. It was a painstaking report, and it had to be accurate. Miss a child, lose a lot of money.

Jeanne found the telephone number of the special services offices and placed a second call to the urban district. "I wanted to alert you that I met this morning with Kathy Baker regarding her son Jason. I believe he was in one of your self-contained classes."

"Okay," said the voice on the other end of the line.

"Mrs. Baker informed me that she is homeless and Jason is living with her stepfather until she finds a place to live."

"Okay."

"She would like to have Jason continue to attend your school. You will need to arrange for his transportation to and from your district." There was no response so she continued, "I thought you would want to get him back in school before the federal application for aid is due."

"Thanks for the information," the person said. "I will refer this to our homeless coordinator." Jeanne was surprised that a district had a homeless coordinator—it was an indication of how many children were in that situation.

The following week, Connie reminded her boss that Jason was still living with his stepfather and was not going to school. Jeanne was surprised since the count date had already passed. No student, no credit, was the iron law of the student count. Last year, a high school student sassed a police officer and ended up in juvenile detention on the day of the count. He was only detained for one day, but the detention center was able to count him for the whole year. Jeanne's district got no federal aid for him even though he was back in the high school resource center the very next day.

Jeanne called the urban district's office of special services again, but this time she decided to follow up with a letter and copy it to Jason's mother at her stepfather's address. She also sent a copy over to the elementary school to keep the principal informed.

When Connie came in to have Jeanne sign the letter, she had a funny look on her face. "What is it?" Jeanne asked, knowing that look.

"They aren't going to do anything for this kid in that crummy district. They have too many kids."

"Hey, Connie, it's the parent's right to choose where to send their kid to school while they are homeless. He has had enough change, at least he should stay with his same school and teacher." Connie replied to her boss with a saucy look that said, "Our schools are better than their schools and this child should come here."

The Xerox machine was whirring the next morning as Connie made copies for Mrs. Gabour. Peter Weitzman, the elementary principal, called.

"Hey Jeanne," he said, much too cheerfully for 8:15 a.m.

"What's up?"

"I got your letter and we got a problem with that homeless kid."

"What's wrong?"

"I know that address."

"So? The laws for the homeless give the parent the right to choose for their children to continue in the old school or to come to the school where they are temporarily living."

"That's not the problem," he sighed. "One problem is that I'm not supposed to tell you what the problem is."

"What?" she said, a little irritated. "You're not making sense." This was unlike Peter; he never teased and he let people know immediately what he thought.

He sighed a long sigh and stared out of his window into the street filled with cars dropping off students. "It has to do with Megan's Law."

"Child molesters?"

"Right. In Megan's Law there are three levels of notification depending on the level assigned to an offender. Under court rulings, warnings must be carefully tailored to reach only those people who are likely to encounter a sex offender. When a person is a tier-III, or high-risk offender, all of the schools and community agencies are notified with a description, the address, and a picture. We are required to share this with our staff and notify parents.

"For a tier-II or moderate-risk offender, I am notified, however, I cannot legally share this information with anyone. For a tier-I or low-level offender, only the police are notified."

"Peter, I work as an administrator in every school in the district. Surely I am part of your administrative team and you can share this with me."

"I don't know," he stammered.

"Oh, cut it out," Jeanne said. "This is ridiculous. So break the law— you can always plead entrapment and I will take the rap." She could not imagine why one administrator could not tell another when a student was involved in such a serious situation.

"Well," he started slowly, then his words ended in a rush. "I just got this flyer from the police last week. I read your letter about the homeless student last night. The address struck my eye and I realized that this student is living with a sex offender."

Peter continued, "A person lives at the address on your letter who is a level-two offender—however I am not authorized to disclose this information to you or anyone else. This person is not allowed within 250 feet of my school." Then he added, "Jeanne, this information is confidential."

"No!"

"Yes, it is. The offender is not the stepfather, it's his adult son."

Jeanne was shocked at this news. "So a little boy with intellectual disabilities is living with a sex offender and he is not even in school! He is there all day every day."

"That is what it looks like," Peter sighed. "Now, Jeanne," he continued, and his voice got very stern. "You are not to tell anyone this information. It is confidential and I don't want to lose my teaching license."

Jeanne hung up the phone and wondered how in the world a mother could drop her son off at the home of a sexual predator and go and live with her boyfriend. She decided to speak directly with the director of special services in Jason's old district. At least if this child was in school he could alert his teacher if something were going on in the home.

Teachers are required to call the Division of Youth and Family Services, if they suspect any kind of abuse. Jeanne was sure that she could make the director understand the importance of getting this young man into school without having to reveal the confidential information. Late that afternoon Jeanne finally reached him.

Like her, he was still in his office well after everyone had gone home. The district was quiet, parents were busy getting dinner on the table and the phones didn't ring. It was a good time to finish reports and prepare new ones for the board of education about why special education cost so much.

Bill seemed receptive on the phone; he didn't argue with Jeanne's pointed comments. She told him, "I can't exactly tell you why, but please understand me—that child needs to be in school." He agreed to see that arrangements were made for Jason to get picked up and transported back to his old school.

The office seemed asleep early Friday morning after a February snow day. Heavy piles of snow littered the streets punctuated by cars. Snow, car, snow, car, car. Only the piles at the end of the macadam playground were still white but; by the end of the day they would be brown too. Climbed on, stamped, thrown around, and cherished by the students, they were despised as dirty and dangerous by the teachers.

Jeanne was in early hoping to attack the piles of individual education plans (IEPs) and child study team reports. Connie arrived, stamping her feet to shake off the snow from her short walk from her home to the school down the street. She had never learned to drive. She hung up her coat and darkened the doorway of Jeanne's office. "I saw that homeless kid outside yesterday without a hat or gloves," she said.

"Who?"

"That homeless kid."

"Oh yeah, I think they set up transportation so he can go to school."

"They didn't; I didn't think they would."

Jeanne sighed, but Connie continued. "My friend Eileen lives across the street from that house. She says he sits in the window looking out all day. She hasn't seen any buses picking the kid up either."

"Shit," Jeanne sucked in her breath.

"Allison only has six kids in her self-contained special class," Connie reminded her. She kept the child count records for the state and knew every single student and where they were. She could check the list for accuracy just by naming all the students. This was a direct hint about what needed to be done for this young man. "You want coffee?"

Connie left to fill the coffeepot so the day could officially begin. Jeanne sat with her chin resting on her fist for a moment and watched the sun break through the clouds for a moment and then disappear. Even a homeless poor kid could not be ignored. She knew about it and would have to do something.

Jeanne could not do anything about getting him out of the home of a child molester—however if he attended school every day he had the opportunity to talk to his teacher if anything was happening at home. His teacher would know if he smelled like sex, or had any bruises, or didn't come at all.

The school district would have some authority about this situation if Jason was attending school. There were always stories in the papers about children who were molested, starved, or beaten. Most of the time they were being homeschooled and out of the reach of people who would notice something wrong.

First Jeanne would have to find his mother's phone number at her boyfriend's or any of the other paperwork about this kid. As Connie passed by she poked her head in to let her boss know that the coffee was ready and she had gotten a carton of fresh milk from the cafeteria.

"I have the paperwork on that kid," she said to the desk because Jeanne was crouched beside it rifling through the carton of files that sat on the floor.

After reaching Jason's mother, Jeanne explained that they wanted to enroll Jason in the district's self-contained program. She explained that he would begin in a special classroom and they would review his program in a few weeks when his IEP and other paperwork arrived from his other district. Kathy said she would to call her stepfather and have him bring Jason over to the school.

Peter Weitzman was not so eager. "Hey, I have to call the prosecutor on this one," he said firmly. "I can't have this sexual predator within fifty feet of my school. Jeanne, I want the kid in school, don't get me wrong, but I have 250 other kids to worry about."

According to the county prosecutor, this was not going to be a simple school registration. The local police precinct captain needed to come or send a designee, the county prosecutor's office needed to be present, the probation officer needed to attend and, if the offender wished to bring an attorney, he or she needed to be present as well.

"Well, when can we meet," Jeanne asked the prosecutor. "I think this young boy needs to be in school as soon as possible. God knows what is going on in that house and that child has no one to talk to."

"Okay, I am in court tomorrow and that case may well take the rest of the week. I could clear something for late in the day next Thursday."

"Hey—it has been three months that this kid will be out of school—we don't have any idea what is going on with him. Why can't we get him in school on Monday?"

Papers were shuffled on the other end of the phone and the prosecutor cleared his throat several times—sounded like a cold. "I don't think you need to get too worried about this kid," he said. "The offender in this case is attracted to young girls, not boys. Most sex offenders do not stray from their profile. Most likely he won't go after a boy."

It was almost two weeks before a meeting could be held. The legal system seemed to have no regard for how many days of school this child had already missed and was still missing. The day before the meeting, the prosecutor's office called to say that he had to be in court the next day. The only time he could attend the tier-II offender meeting would be that very afternoon at four. If Jeanne could not get everyone to attend, it would be another couple of weeks before the prosecutor's schedule cleared.

Determined, Jeanne sat down to man the phones. She could leave her three o'clock IEP meeting at four and let the psychologist finish up with the parents. She called Mrs. Baker and she agreed to go into her job in a bar late that day. "My stepdad don't do nothing anyway, he can come," she said. The police captain agreed that he would be there, and the probation officer agreed as well. However, he wanted to make sure the adult son, the identified offender, understood the rules as well as the stepfather. Both father and son needed to hear the prohibitions against entering a public school.

With a sigh Jeanne finally dialed Peter Weitzman. He, the one person she didn't think would be a problem, sputtered, "I just can't today—why does it have to be today? It's supposed to be tomorrow!"

"The prosecutor has to be in court. If we don't meet this afternoon, then the meeting can't take place for another couple of weeks. We need to get this kid into school. Do you have a parent meeting? Maybe someone else can handle it for you."

"Jeanne," he continued, with a deep, deep sigh. "Do you know what day this is?"

"Tuesday"

"What's the date?" he asked.

"March second."

"What happens on March second?

"Um," she replied. "I don't know."

"It's Dr. Seuss's Birthday."

"Right!" Jeanne said. "I am going over to read to the second graders this morning." Each school celebrated the birthday of this famous author by having local celebrities around town read to the children. The mayor would be in the schools and the superintendent always made the rounds.

Jeanne read the *Cat in the Hat*. In the story, despite their mother's warning about letting anyone in while she was away, her children let a pernicious cat into the house. Jeanne always asked, "Would you tell your mother that you let the cat in?" No one in the first grade would even consider such a thing, but there were usually three or four boys in the second grade who smiled and whispered that they might not tell. By third grade—most children shouted "No, I would not tell!" The one or two silent girls quickly agreed with the rest of the class. By fourth grade no one would tell.

"So what," she said to Peter. "We read during school hours—this meeting is at four in the afternoon. Everyone will have gone home."

"Well, Jeanne, actually," he stammered, then reluctantly revealed, "I'm dressed like the Cat-in-the-Hat." Suddenly, Jeanne understood. Peter had a penchant for costumes, and he would be dressed in short pants with suspenders, black tights, a white shirt, red bow tie, and an amazing striped hat. Everyone in the district looked forward to his various costumes at Halloween and the one-hundredth day of school. His Cat-in-the-Hat outfit was a highlight no one who saw it ever forgot.

"Peter, take the hat, the suspenders, and the bow tie off. Sit behind your desk and don't get up. No one will notice. I will bring everybody in."

"This has to be today?" he signed.

"Yeah, this kid needs to be in school and. . ." she didn't have to continue; Peter interrupted and said that he would be in his office that afternoon.

Fifteen minutes early for the meeting, Kathy Baker appeared with her son. Jason was pale and his blonde hair looked like it had been cut in a buzz that afternoon. He mostly stared at the floor with his hands held between his knees and his leg pushed up against his mother. Jeanne could see that he probably needed to be in a special class. No thirteen-year-old that she knew would sit up close to his mother like that in a public place. He seemed more bewildered than curious, more frightened than anything else.

Mrs. Thomas, the school secretary, mouthed, "He's in his office," to let Jeanne know that Peter was indeed sitting behind his desk and that she knew why. There is little that escapes the stalwart guardians of public schools. Jeanne greeted Kathy, who mumbled that her stepfather and stepbrother were walking over. Jeanne also shook Jason's limp hand. He didn't know quite what to do about that, and the flesh on his upper arm shook back and forth.

The security buzzer rang and while Mrs. Thomas opened the electronic door for the next arrivals, Jeanne went into the inner office to see how Peter was doing. He didn't look bad. He had taken off the hat and the suspenders. All you could see was the white shirt.

For him, it seemed strange since he was always impeccably dressed in a carefully pressed suit and tie—however most people would not notice anything unusual. He was uncomfortable though. Hosting a big meeting without his usual attire was bothering him.

The county prosecutor, a balding man in a shiny suit, was followed by the police chief. The chief declined the offer of a chair and took a stance at the back of the room near the door. Perhaps he was worried there might be an armed robbery and he had to catch the crook, or perhaps he felt that this meeting was small potatoes. Everyone waited a few moments in uncomfortable silence. Mrs. Thomas knocked on the door to let them know that the visitors were in the building and coming up the stairs.

Jeanne was glad she offered to get another chair from the outer office since it gave her a chance to observe Jason's stepfather. He was an old man in ill-fitting pants who pulled himself up the stairs with the bannister. His son, the sex offender, followed behind him, just as slow on the stairs. Jeanne sucked in her breath when she saw them and was glad that no one could hear.

The tier-I sex offender was a special needs child grown older. He was obviously developmentally disabled. He had small slanted eyes, a short stature, short arms, and a small head. His mouth hung open and a line of drool rolled out of the side. His blue jeans were held up with suspenders, and he didn't look like he could tie his shoes. His shirt was almost buttoned correctly. Jeanne wondered if his father had slicked his hair down. Stubble covered his chin but he had managed to shave his cheeks. So this was the dangerous criminal who years ago had lured a little girl into his backyard taken her panties down and touched her.

Father and son stepped into the office with carefully placed steps. Willie B., the offender, sat looking down for the entire meeting. The prosecutor read off a series of requirements. Willie B. could not enter the school or the school yard. He was not to stand within fifty feet of the school day or night. He was not go to the park or any other places where children gathered. "Do you understand?" he asked.

Willie B. didn't respond, and his father said, "Yes, we do understand." The prosecutor accepted that answer.

The entire meeting took about seven minutes. Willie B. and his father got up immediately; this had been a frightening experience for them. Willie had trouble on the stairs going down and held on to the handrail with both hands, placing one foot on the stair then the other before he took another step. His father followed behind.

When the door to the school closed and the security lock clicked shut behind them, Jeanne turned to the prosecutor. "Willie B? He's developmentally disabled. He probably had no idea that he shouldn't touch those little girls. He's not going to hurt anybody."

"I agree; he's retarded all right." He sighed and reached back to grab his bulging briefcase from the chair in the hallway. The handle on one side had ripped and was hanging by a thin band. "I don't think you'll have any trouble," he said, and hurried down the steps and into the late afternoon darkness.

Jason showed up promptly at 8:30 the following morning. He had new pants that were too long and a belt that might have come from his grandfather. It was looped almost two times around his waist. That endeared him to his teacher, who introduced him to her other students as "our new friend."

Jason had difficulty speaking, as if his lips were weak and could not form the words. He leaked spittle when he tried to make entire sentences. He had learned to be silent, another trait that endeared him to his teacher, who enjoyed engaging children more than calming exuberance.

Jeanne was not surprised that his prior district didn't call to ask where their student was—the state attendance reports were completed and it didn't matter where a student attended school on March 3. If you could claim him on November 1, then you got the state aid.

Just before spring break in the middle of April, Mrs. Baker stopped in to the office of special services.

"That homeless lady is here to see you," Connie said. Jeanne wondered if every student had a frozen epithet. Mark the kid who shot the fire extinguisher off in science class, Alex who flushed a kid's shirt down the toilet, Janet who slapped her stepmother and had to go to juvvie.

Jeanne went out to get Mrs. Baker—but she did not want to come and sit in the office. "I just wanted to drop by and let you know that Jason and I are leaving tomorrow morning."

"Are you going back to your old place?" Connie stopped printing out IEPs and peered intently at Mrs. Baker.

"No, we are going out West. I have had it—this place just doesn't work for us."

"You don't know where you are going?"

"Nope—we are getting in the car and seeing where it takes us. Maybe Vegas."

This was such sad news. Jason was in a good educational program. His teacher liked him, he was getting speech therapy three times a week and his speech was more intelligible. He liked learning about money and could make change for a dollar. The gains he had made would be quickly lost if he stopped attending school.

Jeanne suggested that she wait until the end of the school year, but Mrs. Baker brushed off the suggestion. She was packing the car that afternoon and they were leaving. She edged toward the door. Jeanne offered to put together a packet of information about Jason for his new school, but Kathy Baker turned and said she would have the school call to get the records since she didn't have time to wait.

ESSENTIAL UNDERSTANDINGS

- The Family Educational Rights and Privacy Act (FERPA) ensures that parents and students have access to their educational records. This also protects students' right to privacy. Records cannot be released without consent.

- Parents have a right to see and have copies of all school records on their child—however they can be charged for copies. These copies must be made available in a timely fashion.
- When children are homeless, the law requires that they may continue to attend their former school or the school in the district where they are temporarily housed.
- Each year, school districts complete an application for federal aid based on the number of students with disabilities. When the IDEA was passed, Congress established a maximum target of 40 percent of the additional funds needed to meet the requirements of the law. However, funding levels have never come close to this level, and have even dropped in recent years. Districts receive only about 16 percent of the amount needed to provide special services to students with disabilities.
- Institutions for the developmentally disabled were closed rapidly in the early 1970s due to reports of the terrible conditions inside. However, group homes and community placements were never fully funded. Families were left to care for disabled children at home and often without community support. An entire generation of individuals fell through the cracks of this monumental change.
- Megan's Law requires that community members be informed about sexual offenders who live there. There are three levels of notification depending on the level assigned to an offender. Under court rulings, warnings must be carefully tailored to reach only those people who are likely to encounter a sex offender. When a person is a tier-III, or high-risk offender, all of the schools and community agencies are notified with a description, the address, and a picture. Principals must notify staff and parents. Tier-II offenders are shared with school staff. For a tier-I or low-risk offender, the school principal is notified; however, this information cannot legally be shared with anyone.

NINE

Bullies

There is no worse lie than a truth misunderstood by those who hear it.
—William James

Many teachers and parents grew up in a time when children were expected and encouraged to solve their problems with one another. Adults did not intervene unless a physical altercation occurred. As a result, some children were bullied relentlessly because they had learning problems, unusual physical features, or were somehow different from everyone else. Many suffered lifelong consequences.

Recently this hands-off attitude has been reconsidered. Efforts to protect those who are different, and stop bullying, have resulted in legally mandated actions on the part of teachers. Antibullying laws have been written to encompass every single type of harassment, intimidation, and bullying behavior.

A 2009 study by the U.S. Departments of Justice and Education, *Indicators of School Crime and Safety*, reported that 32 percent of students aged twelve through eighteen were bullied in the previous school year. The study reported that 25 percent of the responding public schools indicated that bullying was a daily or weekly problem.

School administrators can no longer ignore behavior that could be construed as bullying. They now know that if adults respond quickly and consistently interfere with bullying behavior, they send the message that such behavior is not acceptable. Research shows that adult response can stop teasing and other incidents over time. However, deciding when a student's actions toward another reaches the level of bullying can be confusing.

The legal definition of bullying includes lengthy descriptions of all sorts of behavior. One could say that the definition of bullying leaves no behavior behind. Any gesture; any written, verbal, or physical act; or any electronic communication, whether it be a single incident or a series of incidents, that is reasonably perceived as motivated by race, color, religion, ancestry, national origin, gender, sexual orientation, gender identity and expression, or a mental, physical or sensory disability, or by any other distinguishing characteristic, could be construed as bullying.

Legally, bullying must be addressed if it takes place on school property or at any school-sponsored function. It is bullying if a reasonable person should know that it will have the effect of physically or emotionally harming a student or damaging the student's property, or placing a student in reasonable fear of physical or emotional harm. Bullying has the effect of insulting or demeaning any student or group of students and creates a hostile educational environment for the student by interfering with a student's education or by causing physical or emotional harm to the student.

Many states require the superintendent of schools to report any acts of violence, vandalism, harassment, intimidation, or bullying at a public board of education meeting. The report includes the number of reports of bullying, the nature of the bullying, the discipline imposed on the student, training conducted, or programs implemented.

A school that fails to respond appropriately to bullying may be violating one or more civil rights laws enforced by the Department of Education and the Department of Justice, including:

Title IV and Title VI of the Civil Rights Act of 1964;
Section 504 of the Rehabilitation Act of 1973;
Titles II and III of the Americans with Disabilities Act;
The Individuals with Disabilities Education Act (IDEA).

A parent, student, guardian, or organization may file a complaint with the Division on Civil Rights of any incident of harassment, intimidation, or bullying. A school administrator who receives a report of bullying, fails to conduct an investigation, and fails to take sufficient action to eliminate it may be subject to disciplinary action.

These laws are specific about what might be construed as bullying, but none are specific about what should, or could, be done to remediate the bully or aid the victim. In our numerically oriented country, the laws are mainly concerned with uncovering incidents of such behavior and making sure they are counted. Mandated interventions would require funding, and that has not been provided.

Students with special needs are at special risk to be bullied and Ali was one such case. He was big boned, over six feet, and two hundred pounds. Easygoing with lush black eyebrows and unruly hair, he was hard to miss. Ali was proud of being a football player. Football was his passion and the source of his self-esteem. He had been a member of the football team since his freshman year in high school. He thrived on recognition by the other players, the horseplay in the hall, and the macho jokes in the locker room.

However, Ali wasn't quick on the field or in the classroom. The coach positioned him carefully during games, worried that he would forget his position in the play. Large in size, he did not possess a large intelligence. He was sweet and kind and, despite the coach's hopes, not an aggressive player. He had trouble remembering the plays and didn't like knocking other players over to get to the ball. However, he was a massive force on the field and, once in motion, was difficult to stop.

In order to receive a high school diploma, students have to pass four years of English, two years of American history, and three years of both math and science courses. These academic courses were not easy for Ali. He had repeated seventh grade and was passed into eighth grade mainly due to his size and age. As a high school junior, he struggled to pass his classes with a C so he could remain eligible for the football team.

Ali had been referred to the special education diagnostic team several times during his early school years. Each time he had been evaluated by a psychologist and a learning disability consultant to see if he qualified for special education services. However, like many others, he had low-average ability as measured by an IQ test, and his academic skills were also in the low-average range.

In order to qualify for special services and protections under the Individuals with Disabilities Education Act, he needed to meet the federal requirements in a disability category. The most appropriate category for Ali was specific learning disability. However, Ali did not have the severe discrepancy between his ability and his performance required by the IDEA.

According to the Individuals with Disabilities Education Act, a specific learning disability means a disorder in one or more of the basic psychological processes involved in understanding or using language, spoken or written, that results in an imperfect ability to listen, think, speak, read, write, spell, or do mathematical calculations. This includes conditions such as perceptual disabilities and dyslexia.

A severe discrepancy applies when a student of average or above-average ability, measured by an IQ test, is not performing academically in the average or above-average range. There is a discrepancy between the student's ability level and their performance level. There was no discrepancy in Ali's case. His ability level matched his academic performance.

Ali had a low-average IQ, but not low enough to be considered mildly cognitively impaired as an IDEA classification. An IQ score below eighty means that a student can be classified as having a cognitive deficit and receive special education services. Ali's IQ score was eighty-three. Each time he was evaluated, Ali didn't qualify for special education services under any of the federally mandated classifications.

His parents did not speak English at home and could not help him with his homework. His father operated a food truck, and Ali often worked long hours on the truck after school and on weekends. Ali's parents were not savvy about how to get special education services for their son, and the school did nothing to educate them. The school administration would be very upset with any teacher who advised parents to bring a special education lawsuit against their school district.

Ali fell further and further behind throughout elementary school and into middle school. He never memorized the times tables and could not estimate a range of answers which made using a calculator problematic. He had a limited vocabulary and struggled with reading comprehension. His school no longer had remedial reading or math programs. Those kinds of supports for struggling students were closed over the years due to budget cuts. Shop classes, home economics, and work study programs were disbanded due to the emphasis on test scores. Teaching a child a trade does not raise test scores.

When he was placed in eighth grade due to his size and age, the high school special education multidisciplinary assessment team evaluated him again. They decided Ali needed special education services and classified him as learning disabled.

Ali did not have a severe discrepancy, but he was failing every single class. Without the protections offered to him by the IDEA, it was certain that he would not finish high school. His classification would allow him to be placed in special education academic resource center classes where he would be taught as his academic level. There was a limit of the number of students who could be in the resource classes.

Ali would have a better chance to graduate from high school due to the protections offered by the IDEA. The multidisciplinary team could exempt him from having to pass the state mandated graduation test. He would need to take it; however, a failing score would not keep him from getting a high school diploma. Even though he would have to take the high stakes testing, his scores would be reported separately. They would not pull down the test scores reported to the community.

Most high schools have several levels of classes ranging from advanced placement, college prep, general education, and finally special education replacement courses. Now that he was classified, Ali could attend the replacement special education courses for English, math, science, and U.S. history. He would be able to pass each course and remain eligible for the football team.

Ali's special education math teacher, Lisa, was eager to work with students like Ali. She was concerned about the number of students with special needs who dropped out of high school. Failing a grade and repeating it was another good predictor of leaving school before graduation. Since Ali had special needs and had repeated seventh grade, he was a good candidate for not graduating from high school. Students can drop out when they turn sixteen with permission from their parents. They can leave school when they are eighteen on their own.

Many of the students in Lisa's special education math class had been held back in earlier grades and were nearing eighteen. They were sensitive about their age and were aware of their limited academic ability. Lisa struggled to find ways to keep them engaged.

She badgered the math department until they gave her the same algebra books that other students used for her students. The chair of the math department needed quite a bit of convincing. He didn't see how students with special needs could handle algebra and thought it was a waste of textbook money.

Lisa knew that her students didn't want to carry fifth-grade textbooks in the hallways. Even if their math skills were at a fifth-grade level, they didn't want to advertise their academic difficulties. Carrying a book others completed in elementary school was humiliating. The standard algebra books were a motivator. Lisa explained to the math department chair that her special education students needed a new attitude about math. They needed to stick with problems that were tough for them. They needed to believe they could be successful. He knew enough about math phobia to understand exactly what she was saying and gave her the books.

Lisa adapted problems from the book to reinforce addition, subtraction, multiplication and division skills. $24a + 24a = 48a$ or $2(24a + 24a) = x$. Students with special needs who had avoided math for years were suddenly interested in equations. Their algebra book was often placed out on the lunchroom table, rather than hidden in a locker or backpack. They carried the books home and showed them to their parents and siblings. It was a sign that said: I am not stupid. I can do this. A positive attitude is the most basic requirement for learning. At the beginning of every class her students chanted: Work harder, get smarter!

Slogans, although helpful, are not enough. Lisa knew that in order to encourage her students to stay in school, they needed to have a plans for their futures. They needed goals and dreams. They needed to believe they could achieve their dreams. They needed to see that a high school diploma, and maybe even a college degree, would help them to reach their goals. First they needed to have some ideas about what they wanted to do with their lives.

Normally developing children are asked repeatedly by parents, uncles, grandma, and the neighbors, "What do you want to be when you grow up?" These questions intensify in high school where parents work with their child to make specific plans. How much will college cost? Can you get an athletic scholarship?

Once a child is identified as handicapped, most of those questions stop. The IDEA was developed on a medical model that emphasizes areas of disability. Strengths are not evaluated and are not included in the individual education plan (IEP) document. This approach was useful in garnering support for special education programs and funding when the IDEA was introduced. However it is a lopsided view of individuals with disabilities. Everyone has strengths as well as weaknesses. The deficit model is harmful.

Parents love their child, but may stop dreaming, planning, and hoping about the future once a child is labeled as handicapped by a professional team. Future plans are replaced with acceptance and lower expectations that are sadly considered realistic.

In order to encourage planning and goal setting, Lisa had each of her students create a "Vision Board": a collage of pictures and words that showed what they wanted to look like and do in the future. She asked everyone to think about their future. She talked with her class about career choices and the education they would need to reach their goals. They looked at salary guides and the cost of cars, motorcycles, and apartments.

Her students cut pictures out of magazines, or drew and wrote about what they wanted to be and do with their lives. Rock stars, coaches, teachers, and ice cream store owners were depicted along with high school and college diplomas, nice cars, and flashy watches. During a class in which she saw someone giving up on a problem or idly looking out the window, Lisa sometimes would just point to the student's Vision Board as a nonverbal, but powerful hint about what they needed to do. She encouraged her students with special needs to remember their vision for the future when they felt frustrated by an academic or personal challenge.

In many conversations with his teacher, Ali could not tell her what he wanted to be. It seemed as though he had never been asked. He didn't know what kind of a job he wanted, but he knew he didn't want to go to school any more than he had to. He thought he might like to be a football player, but understood that was an unreachable goal. He knew he wasn't that good of a player despite his size.

One day, after fruitless questions about his future that only seemed to underscore Ali's limited ability, Lisa asked him to close his eyes. "Imagine what you look like in five years," she said. "Tell me what you are wearing on your way to your job."

Ali answered clearly and confidently. "I am wearing a suit." He wanted a job where he would wear a suit to work each day, "I want to look really sharp," he told his teacher. For Ali, a suit meant that he had achieved something.

Ali created a collage about himself. He included several pictures of men in suits. There were football players and a red sports car in his vision. He wanted a driver's license and a job where he could dress up each day. He didn't want to work on his father's food truck in sweats and a hat.

His teacher thought about this for several days until finally, while out walking her dog, she thought of a suggestion. Ali was big and strong. He was an imposing figure in the hallways. He was also slow to anger and deliberate. Would he make a good security guard in a bank or other business? She wondered if he would consider a uniform instead of just a suit. Starting with the student's ideas and encouraging him, had led to a possible goal.

When Jeanne, the director of special services, strolled into Lisa's classroom one afternoon to say hello, she quietly paused to admire the students' Vision Boards. They were prominently displayed at the front of the classroom. She was pleased to witness how a creative teacher had addressed a major issue for students who struggle academically: motivation.

Research has repeatedly demonstrated that self-control is more important for success in life than IQ, but school programs all seem to equate success with academic ability. Perseverance toward a goal is a key to success, but how to convince adolescents of its value is elusive. Lisa had made this an important part of her academic approach.

In Maslow's hierarchy of needs, self-actualization is the highest level. Here were collages of each student's highest goals, their ideas about self-actualization. The students didn't aspire to own businesses or to be doctors. They wanted to live in apartments, to have girlfriends, to eat in restaurants, or to choose clothes that made them feel good. They wanted to go to football games, take art classes, go to concerts, or travel to Niagara Falls.

Jeanne stopped in front of Ali's Vision Board and suddenly got very angry. Someone had written "ET" in large black letters across the front of it. E.T., the little alien in the movie from the same name, who just wanted to go home. Shocked at this blatant taunt she turned around and glared at each of the students in the room.

Respect for someone's life goals and ambition, no matter how simple, is sacred. How cruel to write an anonymous message that implies the person is from outer space. This was especially true for Ali due to his special needs. It seemed to Jeanne that despite almost a half-century of inclusion, the school community still could not accept students with handicaps. She was shocked that no one had noticed this before.

"Who did this?" she demanded, pointing to the offending letters on Ali's creation. Calling a student names, like alien, from outer space, weird, or even strange, was bullying behavior. It could not be tolerated especially with vulnerable students. Lisa stopped talking about the upcoming test on understanding graphs and stared at the director of special services.

"What is this?" Jeanne asked again. "What exactly is this?" she repeated, pointing to the belittling letters.

Silence.

"I'd like to know, who wrote E.T. on Ali's Vision Board?" she repeated in a louder voice.

Silence.

"Everyone in this room needs to know that this is unacceptable bullying and it will not be tolerated. Calling a student in this school an alien from outer space is not permissible! It is hurtful and mean."

The students in the class remained silent, Lisa, standing near the windows, looked upset. Perhaps she had not noticed the insulting letters.

Slowly, Ali raised his hand. Jeanne gestured for him to come and over and speak with her. She had started to realize that calling attention to this problem while he was present was the wrong thing to do. He was now a double victim, and she wished she had not responded in such a public way.

Ali slowly got up from his desk. He ambled up to the front of the room. Jeanne thought he might know who had written it and she walked him into the hallway where he could talk to her in private. She regretted announcing this to the entire class. It should have been handled in a private way. Like many students with special needs, Ali was eager to be accepted and might not have realized that this was making fun of him. He was easily influenced by others in his wish to have friends. Whoever did this was not his friend.

"Ali, I am so sorry about this," she said. "I will make sure that this does not happen again."

Ali bent down and whispered in her ear, "But I like it."

"Why do you like being called E.T.?"

"That's what everybody on the football team calls me," he said proudly. "It's my nickname."

Jeanne probed, "Well that's not a very nice nickname."

"I like it," he said with a little nod of his head. "I think one of the guys from the locker room wrote it."

"Ali, I won't allow anyone to call you names, it is not nice. E.T. is the name of a little man from outer space. I don't think you are from outer space and I don't appreciate anyone implying that you are. Did you see the movie, *E.T.?*"

"No," he replied slowly. "But that isn't why the guys call me E.T." He suddenly seemed unsure and was obviously wondering what was wrong with the letters.

"Do you know why they call you that?"

Ali's face lit up with a smile, "All the guys on the team all call me E.T.," he said. "So does the coach."

"Oh dear!" Jeanne was shocked to hear that the coach and the entire football team participated in this bullying behavior.

"It's not about a movie," Ali explained shaking his head. He leaned in closer to her with a satisfied look on his face. "Most boys have two testicles, me, I've got three! E.T. means, extra testicle. That's me—E.T. Get it?" Ali smiled broadly and proudly.

Stymied, surprised, and struggling for what to say, Jeanne decided to cut her losses. She stammered, "Okay, now I understand, Ali." She didn't know what to do with this information and walked Ali back into the classroom. She said, "Thanks for sharing," with as much dignity as she could muster. The rest of the class, along with their teacher, tittered. Well, she thought, the helping hand strikes again.

In Ali's mind, an extra testicle was obviously a source of pride, not a problem. But was it appropriate for his fellow teammates to remark on this unusual physical attribute? It is bullying if a reasonable person should know that it will have the effect of physically or emotionally harming a student. Did this nickname benefit Ali or hurt him?

This nickname did not seem to harm Ali; he was proud of it. Jeanne could not decide if this was an incident of bullying or not. Did she need to fill out a report, interview the victim and the perpetrators, and then determine an appropriate course of action? What would the report say? Victim of bullying is proud of his individual differences and appreciates others who reference it.

Ali's teacher had respected his dreams for the future. She did not disagree when he said a major goal in his life was to wear a suit to work. If he felt that E.T. was a good nickname and was proud of it, was that bullying? Jeanne had to consider the possibility of backlash against him if she went to the football coach and reported the nickname. Was it even possible for adults to intervene in a situation like this without making it worse?

When asked about her disability, a young woman with Down syndrome explained, "I have an extra chromosome." She could have been talking about her shoe size or her height. She didn't describe herself as a person with a disability. She saw herself as a unique individual, much as Ali did.

ESSENTIAL UNDERSTANDINGS

- According to the Individuals with Disabilities Education Act, a specific learning disability means a disorder in one or more of the basic psychological processes involved in understanding or using language, spoken or written, that results in an imperfect ability to listen, think, speak, read, write, spell, or do mathematical calculations. This includes conditions such as perceptual disabilities and dyslexia.
- A severe discrepancy applies when a student of average or above-average ability, measured by an IQ test, is not performing academically in the average or above-average range. There is a discrepancy

between the ability level and the performance level. There was no discrepancy in Ali's case. His ability level matched his performance.

- An IQ score below eighty means that a student can be classified as having a cognitive deficit and receive special education services.
- The IDEA allows a multidisciplinary team to exempt students with disabilities from having to pass a mandated graduation test. The Elementary and Secondary Education Act requires that all students be tested and the test scores be made public. Students with disabilities must take state mandated tests; however, a failing score does not keep them from a diploma.
- A 2009 study by the U.S. Departments of Justice and Education, *Indicators of School Crime and Safety*, reported that 32 percent of students aged twelve through eighteen were bullied in the previous school year. The study reported that 25 percent of the responding public schools indicated that bullying was a daily or weekly problem.
- Federal and state laws about bullying attempt to be comprehensive; however, their complexity results in confusion.

TEN

The Helping Hand Strikes Again

If you treat an individual as he is, he will stay as he is, but if you treat him as if he were what he ought to be and could be, he will become what he ought to be and could be.
—Johann Wolgang von Goethe

Children with developmental disabilities were once housed in institutions where they could be protected from mistreatment. Then, they were separated from normally developing peers in special classrooms where they could be protected from the demands of an academic curriculum. Today, they are included in general education programs; however, many are protected by an instructional aide who is with them throughout their school day.

Teachers and administrators are quite naturally concerned with protecting students with special needs. However, does all this protection actually keep them separate from other students? Do individuals with special needs need to fail occasionally in order to solve problems on their own?

Ally put on her vivid pink t-shirt and new pink tennis shoes. She meticulously tied the white laces in a bow. She left the room she shared with her sister and found her mother drinking coffee on the front porch. They were staying at the Veranda House B&B for a few days. Her parents were looking for a summer house to buy on Nantucket Island.

Ally asked her mother if she could go outside and take a walk down to the ferry dock before everyone gathered for breakfast. Megan thought that Ally might be ready to do just that—she had turned thirteen in June and it was time to encourage her independence. The ferry dock was just down the street.

Nantucket is a tranquil elbow of land off the coast of Massachusetts; occasionally the *Island Times* would report vandals had knocked over a

131

mailbox or a cat had gone missing. Megan told her daughter not to be gone too long and assumed she would walk down the hill and over to watch the eight o'clock ferry come in to the dock.

Ally has an unusually rounded face that is perfectly centered in her mother's delicate blonde hair. She also has the enlarged tongue typical of individuals with Down syndrome, which makes it difficult for her to speak clearly. Megan understood her daughter quite well. She watched as Ally walked down the steep stairs with alternating feet and remembered how they had practiced that skill for months and months when Ally was three. She wondered if her sister, Kelly, had suggested the pink top and white shorts. Kelly was always concerned about how her older sister looked, acted, and dressed.

Megan waited for her husband, David, who had already gone out to drive by some potential houses while she listened to the squabbles among the black-backed and the laughing gulls. She enjoyed the view of Nantucket Harbor and read the *Island Times*.

She was beginning to wonder why Ally hadn't come back when Kelly came down to breakfast. A little alarmed about Ally, she confided, "Don't tell your father, but I told Ally she could take a walk by herself about a half an hour ago. She should have come back by now. Let's look for her."

Megan and her daughter walked down the crushed shell driveway. They took opposite directions on the two-lane road that led to the beaches on the left and into town on the right. Ally's pink shirt did not materialize. Megan began to blame herself since she had not checked to see if her daughter was wearing her digital watch and she had not told her exactly when she needed to come back. She realized that Ally might not even know the name of the B&B and she certainly did not know the phone number.

David was puzzled and concerned when he returned and found Megan walking back up the road still looking for Ally. He decided they should walk over to the nearby police station while Kelly explored several of the paths that ran through the salt grass to the beach.

There are fifty physical clinical features of Down syndrome, but not all appear in every individual. Ally had the most common characteristics including a short, stocky stature with broad, short hands and fingers. She was slightly taller than the blowing grass but she might be sitting down to rest or playing in the sand.

At the unpretentious police station, Megan leaned on the Formica countertop to describe her missing child. "My daughter," she said, trying to calm her growing anxiety, "she has Down syndrome and she is wearing a pink shirt and she has been gone over an hour." Megan rushed the words together, but her tone aroused the police officer who immediately got up from a battered desk on the other side of the counter.

She usually didn't mention that her daughter had Down syndrome. This was not something she would say to describe her child. She found

Ally to be consistently kind, patient, and more cheerful than her other daughters. Down syndrome was something Ally had, like impacted wisdom teeth, or poor eyesight; it wasn't something that defined who her daughter was. However, in this situation it was the first thing she could think of to say.

The reaction from the police officer was not what he usually said to parents of children who had wandered away from the family beach towel. He didn't say, "She'll turn up in an hour or so." He turned his head and called two officers from the back room. Given Ally's description, both men immediately set off on trail bikes so they could quickly cover the beach and paths through the blueberry bushes along the bluffs as well as the roads through town.

With panic constricting her throat Megan forced herself to breathe slowly and deeply while she walked down to Children's Beach, hoping that Kelly had found her sister. She looked for Kelly along the shore strewn with sea grapes and twisted driftwood baked so dry it was shining. Megan avoided looking across the water to Tuckernuck Island and blamed herself for not telling Ally to wear her watch and for not slipping the name of the B&B in her pocket so she could ask for directions.

This spring Ally had been asking to do more things on her own. They had argued just before they left for Nantucket when Megan took her daughter to get her hair cut. Ally sat down in the chair at the beauty shop and when Megan started to talk to Sally, the stylist, Ally stretched out her foot to reach the floor and turned the chair around to face her mother.

"I want to do this," she said. "Please go and don't talk to Sally. I know how I want my hair cut." Megan took a little step back and felt her palms get sweaty. She thought she might take Sally aside and talk to her privately to appease her daughter, and then she bit her lip and decided that she would let Ally explain what she wanted to Sally. Ally would have to live with the haircut she requested.

Although it was difficult for her not to say something, this is what she and David had always wanted for Ally; they wanted her to reach her fullest potential and be independent enough to make her own choices. She glanced at Sally who was waiting for a nod, and then she told them she would be back in a half an hour. She strained to hear Ally talking to Sally and she could almost feel the effort Ally was making to use the lip and tongue placements she had learned in speech therapy to enunciate clearly so Sally could understand her.

The ginger-colored sand was a still place between the ocean waves and the waving beach grass, and Megan tried to keep her mind quiet for a moment so she could think. She regretted that she hadn't reviewed safe people to ask for help with Ally. Ally might not remember to go into a store and ask a clerk; she just might talk to someone on the street. Perhaps that is what she had done and had given them her home telephone number. Ally knew her address and phone number at home, but even if she was calm and speaking clearly, she did not know the address of the Veranda House B&B. Megan herself didn't know the phone number.

David's long strides took him through town, and he looked intently into every shop that he passed. His jaw was pinched into a straight line by the time he walked past the video store, Mitchell's Book Corner, and the gift shops along Main Street. He peered through the windows hoping to see a pink t-shirt and walked up and down the aisles in Congdon's Pharmacy. He didn't feel like asking if anyone had seen his daughter, and he didn't recognize the woman resting her elbows on the counter at the checkout.

He went down to the boat docks on Old South Wharf and hoped that Ally hadn't somehow wandered onto the 9:30 ferry that had just departed for Boston. Water Street led past private homes at the edge of town and kept going through the middle of the island before looping around to meander along the moors on the Atlantic shore.

At the last house David was about to double back and ask ferry workers on the docks if anyone had seen a girl in pink. He thought that Ally would not have walked this far and felt she had to be somewhere in one of the shops. Then, on a bench in front of St. Rose's Church, he caught a glimpse of pink. He called his daughter's name, and she turned around to peer at him over the top of the stone bench and called back, "Daddy?"

Back on the sunny porch at the B&B, Ally explained to her relieved family that she had walked down the shell driveway and turned toward town so she could see the boats in the harbor. However when she tried to come back to the bed-and-breakfast, she walked back along a different street and didn't see it. She kept looking for it as she walked along, and she was surprised when she got to the end of the shops. She had been to town many times with her family, and at first she had been pleased to see the shops opening up in the early morning.

She felt okay until she came to the last house, and at that point she realized that she must be lost. "I was getting hungry so I knew I had been gone a long time," she said. "I didn't know what to do and I stood at the edge of the road for a while. I didn't see anybody to ask, and I didn't know if I should talk to someone I didn't know.

"Finally I saw the steeple, and I thought it would be okay if I sat down on the bench in front of the church. I could not think of what else to do so I decided to pray. 'Dear God, please help me. I think I am lost and I don't know what to do.'" Ally smiled and earnestly informed her parents and sister, "That's when I heard Dad calling me. It made me believe in God."

In India many people who practice Hinduism believe that individuals with Down syndrome are actually holy. These are souls who are spiritually advanced, but have chosen to be reincarnated rather than reach heaven. They return to life in order to teach great spiritual truths and help those who are seeking peace, understanding, and an end to human suffering through enlightenment.

Waves of relief and joy washed over Megan as she listened to Ally. Ally brought such happiness to her family. She had a trusting nature. She was never mean or sly. She thought that buzzing bees were very funny and that clouds were fascinating. Her peaceful presence centered everyone in the family. Her loss, for even a few hours, had reminded her mother of how much she brought to their lives.

According to Debra Neubert's 1997 article titled "Time to Grow: The History–and Future–of Preparing Youth for Adult Roles in Society," in 1901, a parent in Chester, Massachusetts, asked that his child with disabilities attend public school. However, the court ruled that "The right of every child to attend public schools is not unqualified but is subject to . . . reasonable qualifications of pupils." This principle of exclusivity determined that educating disabled children was a waste of resources.

It took almost one hundred years until a New Jersey court agreed with parents that an intellectual disability did not preclude a child from attending school in a general education classroom. In 1992 the parents of Rafael Oberti sued their school district because they felt strongly that Rafael, who has Down syndrome, would learn more in regular classes than he would in a program designed for children with intellectual disabilities.

The judge wrote that "inclusion" or attending regular classes is a right, not a special privilege for a select few. Students could no longer be sent to special classes for the disabled based solely on their disability label. If they could benefit from being with normally developing children and did not disrupt the class or take too much of the teacher's time, they had a legal right to attend general education classes. During many days of testimony, Rafael sat quietly in the courtroom. What other evidence did you need?

Ally had attended a special preschool program specifically designed for toddlers with Down syndrome. It was operated by the local group of the Association for Retarded Citizens (ARC). However, her parents wanted her to have the enrichment offered by their neighborhood school, and they were determined that she should be known and accepted by the children and adults in their town. They convinced the director of special education to try a very new kind of special education called inclusion. They asked to have their daughter, like Rafael Oberti, included in general education classes.

Ally was the very first person with Down syndrome to ever attend first grade in her local elementary school; in fact, she was one of the first in the entire country to attend general education classes. The district trained the classroom teachers, provided Ally with a personal instructional aide, and met frequently with her parents to review and adjust her program.

Ally quickly learned to put her coat and her backpack in her cubby, to get in line for lunch and sit on the rug to listen to stories read by the teacher. She went with her classmates from grade to grade in elementary school and then she was old enough to attend the nearby middle school.

The middle school was a new building with spacious rooms and several computer labs. Large round windows in the media center let in light and put the extensive book collection and all of the computer stations on display. Parents and teachers were proud of the beautiful modern school. Students were challenged to excel in academics, sports, and music. The members of the board of education discussed starting algebra in middle school to prepare students for higher mathematics in high school.

Ally's enrollment sent shock waves through the district. It was one thing for a student with Down syndrome to be in the elementary school. The children there were playing with puppets, learning how to count, and drawing elephants. Many thought this "inclusion" thing had gone too far.

Generally speaking, parents are advised by special education personnel to place a child with developmental disabilities into self-contained special education classes at the secondary level even when they have been successfully included at the elementary level. This recommendation is made out of concern for the safety and well-being of the student due to a protectionist attitude about individuals with special needs.

Elementary schools are typically smaller and have more supervision than middle schools or high schools. Children walk from place to place in a well-ordered line; they are not turned loose in the hallways. Teachers are outside with the children before and after school.

A great deal of the resistance to inclusion in secondary schools stems from basic concerns about pupil safety in the larger, more independent setting. Teachers in general, and school administrators in particular, are anxious about anyone who might get lost during the school day while they are responsible for them. Many schools respond to this fear by insisting that a personal aide monitor the student with developmental disabilities at all times. The paraprofessional meets the bus in the morning and puts the child on the bus each afternoon.

In addition to safety, the instructional aide plays another role. Most teachers have not encountered students with developmental disabilities in their general education classes. Most have no training in special education. Successful inclusion requires teachers who are trained in the specific special needs of the individual student and are eager to innovate and improvise for a child with severe disabilities. Due to the complexities of schedules and teacher contracts, it is difficult to ensure this level of participation from teachers at the secondary level where academic content is more abstract and complex.

The paraprofessional or instructional aide sits with the special student in class and is responsible to adapt the material to the level of the student. They are nominally under the supervision of the general education teacher with consultation by the special education teacher; however, most of the student's educational program is actually taught by the instructional aide. Special education administrators are aware of this and try to hire the most competent aides possible; some even hire certified special education teachers.

An unintended consequence may be that the better the aide, the less likely general education teachers and other students are to get involved with the student. Teachers are concerned that students with disabilities will not be able to grasp concepts such as negative numbers or understand Shakespeare. They have little time to adapt assignment papers and tests.

Teachers often assume that adapting assignments for a student with disabilities is the responsibility of the special education teacher. When a competent instructional aide manages to keep a student with special needs quiet and busy in general education classes, everyone else may retreat.

Most parents who request an inclusion program for their child in middle school or high school have experienced times when their child was lost, confused, or upset. Like Ally's parents, they realize that independent problem solving is critical for their child. They are challenging their child to figure things out for themselves at home.

They have found that problem solving is a critical skill for their child and many are comfortable with the idea that their son or daughter may get lost on the way to gym, forget their books, or not be able to open their locker. They prefer to have teachers intervene only if the problem continues. They don't expect or want teachers to make sure problems never happen. They accept that their child doesn't understand parts of what is taught and are interested in incidental learning.

With determined, supportive parents and a court case backing them up, Ally was the first student with a developmental disability registered for classes in the middle school. Her family and the school district's placement team had agreed on a schedule with a combination of general and special education classes.

Ally walked with her instructional aide, Mrs. Helmond, from English to science and social studies. She and Mrs. Helmond always sat at a table in the back far enough away from the other students so their whispers would not disrupt the class. Ally watched the teacher at the front of the room. She did not bother the teacher or the other students.

When someone asked Ally to show them what she was working on, she looked back and forth from her paper to the face of her instructional aide, Mrs. Helmond, for reassurance. Mrs. Helmond taught Ally English, math, science, and social studies depending on the class. Ally walked with her personal aide in the hallways while the middle school students shouted and chattered as they passed by.

The middle school teachers did not seem to mind having Ally in their classes, why should they? Ally and Mrs. Helmond had two chairs and space at a table in the back of the room. Ally entered and left without bothering them. Her aide adapted what was going on in the class to something that Ally could do. She told the teacher what grades to put on her report card.

In social studies class while the class studied the Declaration of Independence, Ally colored a picture of the American flag. Mrs. Helmond held red and blue crayons and she handed the correct color to Ally as she pointed to each stripe. When she was asked if she liked to color, she said, "Yes." When asked to count the stripes, Mrs. Helmond took her finger and pointed to each stripe as they counted to thirteen together. When Ally was asked if she knew who raised the flag in front of the school each morning, she whispered and her reply was not audible. Mrs. Helmond realized that Ally didn't arrive until after the flag was already flying and didn't know who put it up or took it down.

Mrs. Helmond met Ally at the bus in the morning and put her back on the bus in the afternoon. She walked Ally to the cafeteria and followed her through the lunch line putting a carton of milk and a slice of pizza on her tray. When Ally wanted to open her milk carton, she looked back over her shoulder and Mrs. Helmond, standing by attentively, put her arms over Ally's shoulders and opened it for her. One of the lunchroom aides stood behind Ally while Mrs. Helmond had her lunch break. The lunchroom aide made sure she didn't wander away or get lost.

In the cafeteria Ally was at a table with several girls from her class. She ate as they chatted with equal exuberance about the new social studies teacher, blue nail polish, and candy pacifiers. When Ally sat down, everyone said hello, but Ally was not drawn into the conversation. The girls at her lunch table had been carefully selected to participate in a friendship group with Ally called a *Circle of Friends*.

The group was composed of seven to eight volunteers who got out of class to meet with Ally and Rose, her case manager, every other week. They listened to the things Ally wanted to do and volunteered to eat lunch with her and watch out for her in the hallways between classes. The group had little parties in school for birthdays and holidays such as Halloween.

One morning just after Christmas, Rose and Jeanne, the director of special services, were standing in the hall waiting for the students to gallivant into their next class before they went into a meeting. Ally and Mrs. Helmond passed by and turned into the English classroom at the end of the hallway.

"Why does Mrs. Helmond carry Ally's books?" Jeanne asked. "Wouldn't it be better if Ally did that?" There was nothing wrong with Ally physically, and a little weight-bearing exercise would be good for her.

Every child in special education programs is assigned a case manager to coordinate their programs and intervene if problems occurred. Rose was one of the most conscientious; she knew her students and she knew their teachers well. She usually didn't appreciate suggestions from administrators who dropped by every now and then. Rose replied, "I think Ally needs to have both hands free so she can open her locker."

"Why can't Ally can put her books on the floor and pick them up again like the other kids?" Rose did not answer; however, a week later, Jeanne happened to see Ally in the hall. She was carrying her own books and Mrs. Helmond followed behind. She stopped Mrs. Helmond and Ally walked on to her class by herself. "How is Ally doing carrying her books?"

"She didn't have a problem. That worked out quite well," Mrs. Helmond said.

"Why not let her get from class to class by herself?" her director asked. "Surely she must know where to go by now. She's been in this school for almost two years." Mrs. Helmond thought Ally could do it, but she was concerned that if she got lost and was late to class, the teachers would think she was not doing a good job.

Each week the director of special services met with the two psychologists, the learning disability teacher consultants, the social workers, and a speech and language specialist to discuss the children in the programs. In addition to conducting evaluations to determine eligibility for special education, each person was a case manager for forty to fifty classified students. It was the time when team members gathered together for an in-house problem solving session. Deep thinking and inspiration were supported with dessert at the scarred oak table in the private conference room.

It was a time and place to critically consider what was being done to meet the unique needs of students with handicapping conditions. One afternoon, Jeanne began to discuss her concerns that in the zeal to include students with developmental disabilities, they might be helping them too much and creating learned helplessness. "How long has Mrs. Helmond been Ally's instructional aide?" she asked.

"Five years, I think," Rose said. "As long as I have been here. Mrs. Helmond came up with Ally from the elementary school and she is excellent. As long as Mrs. Helmond is there, we don't have any problems. Ally likes her, her parents like her, and Mrs. Helmond adores Ally. She would do anything for her. It's a perfect arrangement!"

"But most kids don't stay with the same teacher year after year," the director countered. "Do you think that Ally has become overly dependent on her instructional aide?"

"No, Ally needs her and she makes this inclusion program work. Mrs. Helmond knows everything about Ally and doesn't let her get away with anything. She makes her work."

Perhaps what had been created was the opposite of inclusion. Ally walked around the middle school in a safe little bubble-world. She attended a private little school with one teacher and one student. If the ultimate goal was for Ally to be a productive member of the community, then she would have to deal with many different people, not just the ones who knew her and cared about her.

Mrs. Helmond understood Ally's speech and would interpret for her when others had a difficult time. There was not much interaction between Ally and the other students. The other teachers seemed rather oblivious to the dynamic duo seated in the back of their classrooms.

Jeanne leaned away from the table and said, "I think Ally may be getting too dependent on her aide. She needs a change and perhaps we should consider another aide for next year." She told Rose that she would come to the annual review meeting where the program for the following year was presented to parents.

Each year school districts have a meeting or annual review for every child who is classified with special education needs. Parents are invited to come and confer with their child's teachers about the educational gains that have been made and what the educational program should look like in the following year. Agreements made at this meeting are written into a legally binding individualized education program (IEP), which is implemented for the child.

When Jeanne told Rose, Ally's case manager, that she would like to attend her annual review meeting, Rose immediately wanted to know why she wanted to be there. Most directors cannot attend all of the meetings that occur and only come when a difficult problem presents itself. Rose was surprised because everyone in the school was content with Ally's program.

Not only was Rose upset, but the other members of the special education teams basically howled in support of Mrs. Helmond. They were annoyed that a program that was working so well was being made into another problem for both them and for Ally.

Rose was especially vehement. She felt that Ally was making good progress with Mrs. Helmond, who worked hard with her. Why would anyone make a change? Rose calmly assured the director that Ally's parents would never agree to another aide and might take this to court. She reminded the director that parents can have input on the child's program. Parents cannot specify what personnel they wanted for their child, but Ally's parents would be very unhappy. If the district went to court over this idea, it was very likely that they would lose.

Jeanne got the message. The team members had pulled the Individuals with Disabilities Education Act (IDEA) trump card; legal action. They warned the director that her proposal was going to meet major resistance and that she had better back down. Rose left the meeting that afternoon with a parting shot at the director, "Why are you making problems?"

What was the point of making Ally's program more difficult for her when everybody was happy? However, it seemed that in everyone's efforts to ensure Ally's success, they had overprotected her. Ally wasn't included in the middle school; she had her own school. Mrs. Helmond shadowed her from class to class and kept her busy all day long. The teachers taught the general students; Mrs. Helmond taught the included student.

There were many facets that would be impacted by a change in Ally's program. Each student had seven middle school teachers, not one like in elementary school. The teachers were pressured to prepare students for state testing and high school, especially in a suburban district. They were accommodating as long as Ally did not interrupt their classes, and Mrs. Helmond made sure that would not happen.

Would a new aide be too stressful for Ally or would she become a better problem solver? Would academic progress be sacrificed to encourage more interactions among Ally and her classmates? One of the best aspects of the IDEA is that all decisions are made as a team that includes the child's parents. No one person can determine what a student's program will be. Usually you can count on the collective wisdom of parents and the teachers to make good decisions for children with special needs.

It is often dangerous to put a forkful of chicken curry in your mouth without tasting a little bit of it first. The chilies can be so hot that you must leap up and run outside around the restaurant to keep from screaming. It is much better to dip one tine of the fork into Indian food and carefully place a tiny bit on the tongue. Later that week, Jeanne decided to tip a fork tine into "Ally curry" and see how hot it was, when she saw Ally's mother at a parent meeting. After the meeting she approached Megan and asked, "How're we doing?" like Ed Koch when he was the mayor in New York City. "How are we doing with Ally at the middle school?"

Disability is an equal opportunity employer. Any family, rich or poor, strong or tenuous, can have a child with a disability. Some parents pushed the school in new directions like inclusion, and they pushed themselves to create opportunities for their child as well. Others demanded concessions and special programs from the district but sent feverish children to school and left uneaten sandwiches and a plethora of notices at the bottom of their child's backpack.

Ally's family helped her with her homework, made sure that she wore a blue shirt on school spirit day, and enrolled her in skating lessons and taught her to order from a menu. Megan attended every school meeting and was active with the National Down Syndrome Society.

"She is always happy to get on the school bus in the morning," Megan replied, alert and respectful of her daughter's needs and wishes. Staff frequently commented about what parents said and did, rarely about what they wore and how they dressed. Megan however was noted because she managed to be both elegant and casual at the same time.

"What do you think of Ally's aide?" Jeanne continued to probe.

"She is a wonderful woman, and I think she is devoted to my daughter."

"How long has she been working with Ally?"

"Well, for quite a few years now. She came with her when Ally moved from the elementary school to the middle school. "

Jeanne explained that she was concerned that Ally knew Mrs. Helmond too well and asked her for help, even when another student might be very happy to help her. She said that she was afraid that Ally was actually isolated because Mrs. Helmond was so good. "What you would think about having Ally work with someone else next year?" she threw the question out and studied Megan carefully for her reaction. A suggestion about changing staff assignments is a lot like toothpaste. Once you squeeze it out of the tube, it is quite impossible to get it back in.

"That is probably a good idea," Megan said with a smile. "Ally has to remember to enunciate when she speaks and people who know her get used to the way she talks so she forgets to speak clearly. David and I want her to be challenged!"

Megan told Jeanne about the time Ally got lost on Nantucket. That experience had helped her to learn that Ally was going to get lost at times and that it was important for her to do just that. After that incident Ally had written the phone number of where they were staying on little slips of paper and passed them out to everyone, including her mother. Megan also shared that Ally had told her she could hear the clomp, clomp, clomp of Mrs. Helmond's shoes behind her everywhere she went.

The topic of changing Ally's aide was introduced at her annual review meeting. When challenging Ally to go from class to class on her own and reducing her reliance on her aide was suggested by the director of special education, the middle school teachers opposed the suggestion. They felt that because Ally was doing well, her personal aide should not be changed. Ally's parents, however, were comfortable with challenging their daughter. If she got into some sort of difficulty, they felt this was part of learning.

Parents often feel they have little power to influence school programs for their children. However the family's wishes regarding protection versus challenge is critical. In this case the parents had a major impact on the school program without knowing it. The teachers quite naturally were concerned with protecting Ally. They needed the explicit support of her parents to allow her to "get lost" and figure out how to get from class to class on her own. They needed permission to allow Ally to sit with other students, to get the answers wrong, and to wait until the teacher could help her.

Once Ally's parents supported the idea, the teachers agreed that Ally's aide needed to change. After Megan said that she wanted Ally to learn to ask people for help, several teachers felt comfortable enough to admit that they thought Ally was too dependent on Mrs. Helmond; she did not seek out anyone else to help her solve a problem. She basically waited for Mrs. Helmond.

Both David and Megan felt that their daughter should have as much exposure to the regular life of a middle school student as possible. If she got lost or had trouble communicating, they felt that was part of life. If Ally became upset at times, they would accept that as part of growing up. The team decided that beginning that very next week Ally would go to and from all her classes and the bus on her own. She would be taught to go down to the main office if she got lost or her bus was late.

Ally, a full member of the review team, agreed with a little smile. She was proud that everyone recognized that she knew her way around the school and could get from class to class on her own. She asked if she would still see Mrs. Helmond next year, when the aide assignments would change.

It was decided by the IEP team that she would alternate with two aides for the next school year. Mrs. Helmond would be in her English and social studies class and another aide would be assigned in other classes. She would not have an aide in her special education class in math, but would be expected to participate in this small class on her own.

Once her parents supported the transition to a new aide, her case manager and the teaching staff quickly supported the idea. They even revealed their own concerns that Ally and Mrs. Helmond had grown too close and too content with each other's company.

When the new program was implemented, Rose noticed something different. The more Ally moved about the building on her own, the more the girls in her friendship group watched out for her. They were protective in the hallways and seemed to notice Ally there for the first time. They often offered to sit next to Ally during classes and help her understand parts of the lesson. They included her in conversations at the lunch table. A new and better aspect of "protection" had emerged in the school. We are all our brother's (or sister's) keepers.

ESSENTIAL UNDERSTANDINGS

- Inclusion began with efforts to get students with special needs into general education environments with typically developing peers. It focused on where children were educated.
- This was followed by questions of how best to support students in the general education environment. What supports and programs did they need to be successful? The primary focus has been on where students with intellectual disabilities received their education and how to support their success in that environment.
- Occasionally in efforts to protect students, teachers and instructional aides become overprotective. They may limit a student's ability

to practice problem solving skills in a protected environment. Well-meaning aides are eager to do a good job, but what is a good job?

- Although parents do not have a right to determine which teacher will be assigned to their child's program, the opinions of parents matter a great deal to teachers and in the success of an educational program.
- New thinking questions the deficit model and conceptualizes the idea that within an individual, limitations coexist with strengths.
- An important element in an individualized and strength-based total education program is self-determination. Students should take an active role in planning for their future. They need to be encouraged and expected to be causal agents; someone who makes things happen in his or her life.
- Students with special needs must be allowed to get lost, to fail, and to learn from these experiences.

Bibliography

Board of Education of Cleveland Heights v. State ex. Rel. Goldman, 1934. 47 Ohio App. 417, Ohio Ct. App. 1934.

Carrie Buck v. John Hendren Bell, Superintendent of State Colony for Epileptics and Feeble Minded, Citations 274 U.S. 200 47 S. Ct. 584; 71 L. Ed. 1000; 1927 U.S. Lexis 20.

Guest, Kenneth J. 2003. *God in Chinatown: Religion and Survival in New York's Evolving Immigrant Community.* New York: New York University Press.

Miller, S. A., and Stephen Dinan. 2014. "Illegal Border Children Taxing Resources Inside U.S. Schools." *Washington Times,* September 3, http://www.washingtontimes.com/news/2014/sep/3/influx-of-illegal-immigrant-children-presents-chal.

Neubert, Debra. 1997. "Time to Grow: The History of Preparing Youth for Adult Roles in Society." *Teaching Exceptional Children,* May/June, p. 8.

New World Encyclopedia. Online encyclopedia.

Perkins, David. 1995. *Outsmarting IQ: The Emerging Science of Learnable Intelligence.* New York: Free Press.

About the Author

Jeanne D'Haem, PhD is an associate professor of special education and counseling at William Paterson University. Her career in education began as a Peace Corps volunteer in Somalia, East Africa. She was a director of special services and a special education teacher for over thirty years. She lectures widely on issues in special education. She has published two prize-winning books and numerous journal articles. *The Last Camel* (1997) won the Paul Cowin prize for nonfiction. *Desert Dawn* with Waris Dirie (2001) has been translated into over twenty languages and was on the best-seller list in Germany for over a year where it was awarded the Corine prize for nonfiction.